*A Season to Remembe.*

# BURNLEY
## 1959/60

From left to right, back row: Fenton, Blacklaw, Furnell, White. Middle row: Harris, Cummings, Elder, Seith, Miller, Angus, Talbut, Marshall. Front row: Connelly, McIlroy, Adamson, Pointer, Robson, Pilkington.

*A Season to Remember*

# BURNLEY
# 1959/60

*Bill Evans*

TEMPUS

# For Clair and Anne

Lovely daughters who never liked football but still encouraged me

First published 2002

Tempus Publishing Limited
The Mill, Brimscombe Port,
Stroud, Gloucestershire, GL5 2QG

British Library Cataloguing in Publication Data.
A catalogue record for this book is available from the British Library.

ISBN 0 7524 2734 2

Typesetting and origination by Tempus Publishing Limited
Printed in Great Britain by Midway Colour Print, Wiltshire

# Introduction

## When Burnley won the League

At the beginning of the 1950s, Burnley had its own building society, a First Division football team, coal mines which broke new records for production every month, at least sixteen cinemas, countless textile mills, hundreds of chimneys belching out filthy smoke and some of the worst slums in the United Kingdom. There was no unemployment and a third of the population was employed directly by the cotton mills.

As the decade progressed, the slump in the textile industry took its toll and the town's population fell as people left to look for work elsewhere. In one three-month period, one fifth of the working population was made redundant. There was little available in the way of state benefits and many families lived off tinned food, which was cheaper than the fresh equivalent.

In the mills, accidental deaths and injuries weren't uncommon. In one case a man was seriously injured because a machine guard was missing. The mill owners were fined a derisory £10. Another man was killed when he was caught in the main loom belt and hurled up to the ceiling.

Sadly, the management and owners failed to understand the economic climate. A Burnley cotton manufacturer, Mr T. Burrows, when he addressed Burnley Rotary Club, made what must rank as the most misinformed forecast ever – at least until John Bond suggested that under his guidance Burnley would win the League Championship. He said that 'the cotton industry will come through and remain a staple industry not only of Lancashire, but also of the rest of the country.'

The people of Burnley suffered. The town had some of the worst housing in the land, one of the highest rates of suicide and a depressing procession of cases of child neglect coming to the courts. However, one thing that made life a little more bearable was the success of the town's cricket and football teams. It isn't just nostalgic memory that makes eyes mist over at talk of the likes of Jimmy McIlroy and Ray Pointer. Some amazing feats were performed by these heroes. In cricket, Cec Pepper – Burnley's demon bowler – took all ten wickets twice in a fortnight as Burnley claimed a league and Worsley Cup double.

In 1950, a certain butcher called Bob Lord was elected to serve on the board of Burnley Football Club. Star player Harry Potts left the club and the *Burnley Express* bemoaned the fact as his replacement seemed totally inadequate. The *Express* urged the club to buy a new player as no one could replace the great Harry. The would-be replacement failed to make his mark and the club was roundly criticised in many circles for trying to replace the great man with a slightly built youngster. Within a couple of weeks the *Express* changed its tune when the raw young replacement ran Aston Villa ragged. Potts's replacement was a handsome, softly-spoken young Irish lad called Jimmy McIlroy.

Incidentally, the entire Burnley Football Club wage-bill for the year, including everyone from players to administrative staff, was less that £25,000. That would be less than a week's wage for one of today's stars and remember, Burnley were one of the country's top teams. To watch them you could buy a season ticket for less than half the price of a ticket for one match in 2002. A season ticket for a juvenile cost £1.50 – less than today's price of a programme!

The Clarets were building the team that, after Potts returned as manager, would take the title in 1960. Throughout the decade, Burnley FC flew the flag in the top division. The three names – Potts, Lord and McIlroy – would be intertwined throughout the most successful period in the history of the small-town club when a depressed population was cheered by the exploits of their heroes in claret and blue.

Away from football, the Minister of Housing announced slum clearance plans for Burnley, which he stated had the worst slums in the whole of Lancashire and the worst record for building new council houses in all of the Lancashire County Boroughs. At the end of the 1950s the town was ready to sweep away the slums; the building society claimed to be the biggest in the world; the new shopping centre and bus depot were being constructed; and the grammar school continued to be the traditional seat of learning but was now housed in a new, modern building. Television had arrived to stay; many of the cinemas had closed with the arrival of television and most of the factory chimneys stood as redundant black memorials to a dead industry. It had been a period of massive and difficult change.

This then was the background to the period when Blackpool, Bolton, Preston North End and Blackburn Rovers featured with Burnley in League and cup triumphs. It was soccer country and each team had its heroes – Matthews at Blackpool, Finney at Preston, Lofthouse at Bolton and Douglas at Blackburn were all players who would feature on the world football stage.

Like most of my friends, I was a fanatical supporter of Burnley. We would sit with the old men and complain that the Burnley directors weren't ambitious enough when we were seventh in the top division. All my spare moments were spent at Turf Moor, the home of the Clarets, catching players for autographs,

Burnley v. Blackburn Rovers. From left to right: Bennion, Potts, Cummings and McDougall watch from the bench.

watching them train and, most of all, going to the matches where I paid 1s 3d to watch the gods in claret take on the rest of the country. Even now, when I'm introduced to one of the old stars, I feel a childish desire to ask for an autograph.

My obsession with football started when I went to watch a local league game on the cinder pitch in an area of Burnley named Whittlefield. For the benefit of those readers who are not of a certain age, I must explain what cinder pitches were. They had goalposts and nets and they were the regulation football pitch size – but that was about all they had in common with what we recognise today as football pitches. Why? The answer's simple – they had no grass, just a cinder surface.

Cinder pitches taught defenders the art of timing the tackle and forwards the art of avoiding it more effectively than ten years of training. A mistake in timing meant a slide on sharp cinders which would tear the skin to shreds. I'll bet that there are many people who still bear the scars and tell-tale blue specks of cinders buried under the skin on their thighs obtained from unplanned contact with a cinder pitch. Cinder pitches were horrendous, yet football of a very high quality was played on them by local league teams.

Anyway, I digress. As a child, probably aged seven or eight, I went to watch Prestige (a local factory team) and was totally in awe of the players who were kitted out in bright tangerine strips. They won 3-1 and I was hooked on football. When I couldn't actually watch Burnley, I purchased the *Pink* – a local football paper which came out on a Saturday night with all the reports from the matches of the day – and I kept a scrap-book covering every game. The scrap-book was the basis for this publication. Match reports written in laborious long-hand and faded pink-and-black photographs, often blurred and indistinct.

Cinder pitches, clogs, factory chimneys and fog. It was a world which all but disappeared in the 1950s, but through all this change Burnley Football Club remained in the top flight and as the austere Fifties gave way to the brash new Sixties, they reached the pinnacle of achievement by lifting the Football League Championship. The town rejoiced and even those people who professed no interest in football felt a pride in the fact that their small-town team had beaten the likes of Manchester United and Arsenal. The Mayoress joined in the celebrations and telegrams arrived from all over the world.

The Lady Mayoress celebrates with the League Championship-winning team. From left to right: Robson, Miller, Adamson, the Lady Mayoress and Cummings raise a toast to Burnley's success.

# About the Author

In the meantime, my non-football family was moving to Bury. It was assumed that my affair with the club would simply fade away. Not so. Forty years on, I travel from North Wales – a round trip of 200 miles – to watch every match at Turf Moor.

There are so many exiled fans who travel enormous distances to watch Burnley. I know people who come from Plymouth, London, Newbury and Ireland. No one has ever explained why Burnley should be so devoted to its football club and my theory is that the team was always there in the hard times, promising success and achievement amongst so much gloom. A place for hopes and dreams in a time when there was precious little to hold on to. I also believe that Burnley, as Jimmy McIlroy has often said, is one of the friendliest places on earth. Why else would nearly all of the championship squad still live in or near the town?

On a population basis, almost one in nine people in Burnley are season-ticket holders and wherever my travels take me, I meet exiled Claret fans who are keen to hear what's happening at Turf Moor. After my first Burnley book, I had letters from all over the world – India was the furthest – and one gentleman from Cyprus wrote to say how much he enjoyed it.

# Acknowledgements

I've had a great deal of support during the writing of this book. The Burnley Reference Library staff have been brilliant and Howard Talbot has been enthusiastic, patient and unflappable – as well as providing some superb photographs. The *Burnley Express* was always helpful and James and Becky at Tempus were great.

So, after a gap of over forty years, here it is. The Championship year.

Bill Evans
Fordoun Cottage
Llandynan

# HEATED EXCHANGE

**22 August 1959**                    **Leeds United 2 Burnley 3**
Referee: Mr R.T.E. Langdale          Attendance: 20,233

The players emerged from the tunnel at Elland Road into baking heat on the opening day of the season. The country was in the grip of a heatwave which added a carnival atmosphere to the curtain-raising match. Shirtsleeves replaced jackets and knotted handkerchiefs replaced caps as supporters from both sides soaked up the sun.

Referee Langdale blew the whistle to signal the start of the season and Leeds looked the better unit in the opening period as both teams strove to produce excellent football in the suffocating conditions. Leeds had placed a permanent guard of three players on Jimmy McIlroy but even with this close and none-too-gentle attention the mercurial Irishman began to weave his magic and the balance of power started to change.

McIlroy was an elegant, thoughtful player but he was also able to take care of himself when the going got tough and it was clear that the Leeds left half Cush had been given instructions to mark Mac – in all senses of the word. The physical battle continued throughout the game and a draw was about the right result. The skill battle, however, was won comprehensively by the man in claret and blue.

If McIlroy was the star, then he was ably supported by Tommy Cummings, who had a superb game, reading every move. Miller was given the job of marking centre forward Shackleton, who had only recently moved to Leeds from Burnley and 'Shack' responded to Miller's robust marking by flattening several of his ex-colleagues before being taken to task by referee Langdale.

It was Pilkington, the smallest man on the pitch, who opened the scoring when a pass from Jimmy Robson was deflected and landed at his feet. It was an invitation that Pilky didn't spurn and goalkeeper Burgin was given no chance as the ball sped past him.

Burnley were showing their superiority – at times they bordered on the arrogant – and Leeds were looking second-best in all departments. Pointer and Pilkington missed chances before Cummings gathered a loose ball deep in the Burnley half and passed to McIlroy who, realising that Cush was bearing down on him released the ball to Pointer and then ran on to receive the return. A deft flick by Pointer sent the Irishman away again and he beat a defender before passing to Pilkington who immediately returned the ball. McIlroy accelerated past Charlton before passing to Connelly who shot, saw the ball rebound and scored at the second time of asking.

Leeds were down and Burnley surged forward. Poor Jack Charlton was unable

Blacklaw is put to the test in training.

Gordon Harris.

# LEEDS UNITED v. BURNLEY

to take the heat and after having a cold wet sponge administered to him by his trainer he left the pitch, returning later on the left wing.

The second half saw Leeds come back into the game when Bobby Seith suffered a moment of heat-induced madness and flattened Meek in the penalty area with a badly-timed tackle. Cush strolled up the pitch and after placing the ball on the spot he paused for some time, then took a long run and struck his shot past Blacklaw to pull a goal back for the Yorkshire team.

The goal provided only brief respite for Leeds. Pilkington had by now subdued Ashall and he skipped past the full-back, leaving him gasping the hot air like a landed fish and centred for Pointer to meet the ball sweetly and score number three.

Burnley were in total control but perhaps the heat told in the dying minutes as Leeds were allowed to score the most curious of goals. With time ticking away, Don Revie passed to Jack Charlton on the wing and the Burnley defence appeared to be totally unconcerned. The big Geordie simply waltzed into the area, ignored by the Burnley defenders and still without challenge, he scored.

After the match the Burnley players were adamant that the ball had gone out of play long before the shot but referee Mr Langdale didn't agree.

The last few minutes were endured by the two exhausted teams. Leeds couldn't summon up a threat and Burnley were happy to sit back and claim the two points.

A player who would have a vital role in the Burnley Championship season was injured on the opening day in the reserve match at Turf Moor where Burnley beat Leeds by two goals to one. Trevor Meredith fractured his shin with the season only thirteen minutes old. The injury kept him out of contention until the latter part of the season when he returned to replace the injured John Connelly. Meredith scored the goal in the last game of the season which ensured that the Championship went to Turf Moor.

---

**Leeds United**: Burgin, Ashall, Hair, McConnell, Charlton, Cush, Humphries, Revie, Shackleton, Crowe, Meek.
**Burnley**: Blacklaw, Angus, Cummings, Seith, Miller, Adamson, Connelly, McIlroy, Pointer, Robson, Pilkington.

**Scorers:** Connelly, Pointer and Pilkington.

# GOOD DAY

**25 August 1959**
Referee: unknown

**Burnley 5 Everton 2**
Attendance: 29,192

Brilliant weather, brilliant match and, for Burnley, a brilliant result. It had every-thing the perspiring crowd could wish for – seven goals, a fine fight-back and two teams playing skilful, open football, yet the first few minutes were a scrappy affair as the competitors probed and tested their opponents' strengths. The two generals – Bobby Collins of Everton (later to inspire Leeds United in their return to the top flight) and Jimmy McIlroy – tried to gain control and the outright winner was the Burnley man, who linked superbly with Adamson to create numerous openings for his colleagues. Robson, Connelly and Pointer had all missed chances when Pilkington centred from the left corner flag and Robson volleyed goal number one.

Burnley were irresistible as they surged past the royal blue shirts of the Merseysiders. The match was less than twenty minutes old when Burnley were three up. First Pilkington dived into the box to head past Dunlop and then the same player intercepted a poor clearance and beat Jones before passing to Pointer, who had the simple task of slotting the ball home.

Everton were shell-shocked and looked ripe for a drubbing but they scored against the run of play when Collins passed to Thomas, who hit a hard drive past Blacklaw. Suddenly their spirits revived and they came back into the game. The play began to swing from end to end with both forwards spurning chances and Dunlop in the Everton goal saving well on several occasions, notably from Pilkington and Connelly. Blacklaw, too, had his work cut out and he saved acro-batically from Thomas.

McIlroy bamboozled the defence and let rip with a scorching drive which scraped the bar, then Everton swept forward and Blacklaw was charged heavily and fell injured in the area, only for the referee to let play continue. A shot flashed at the Burnley goal and there was Tommy Cummings on the line to half-clear the ball, which fell to Harris who fired wide with the empty goal at his mercy. The main threat to Burnley was expected from the man dubbed Everton's golden boy, Dave Hickson, but he was kept firmly in check by Brian Miller and Everton had to cope without his opportunist style of play. As the whistle blew to end the first half, Burnley were in control and 3-1 was a comfortable lead.

The second half saw Everton press hard to reduce the arrears and the fans applauded their fighting spirit, but just as Everton appeared to be in the ascen-dance, McIlroy controlled the ball midway into the Everton half and beat Meagan and Jones before crossing for Robson to score. Four goals to one. Surely it was all over now.

# BURNLEY v. EVERTON

Robson fights an airborne duel.

Not according to spirited Everton who laid siege to the Burnley goal. Hickson had moved out to the wing to avoid the attentions of the robust Miller and the ploy paid off when he centred for O'Hara and Miller, half-intercepting, headed against his own crossbar. The ball bounced down and was cleared but the referee was adamant that it had crossed the line and a goal was awarded, signalling all-out attack by Everton. The Clarets dropped back and defended resolutely but Hickson had a chance with a powerful header which was well saved by Blacklaw and, in spite of the score-line, Everton were the team who were dominating the match.

Most people in the crowd felt that it was a matter of time before Everton scored but with time running out, Robson gained possession and ran with the ball before passing to Connelly who was running into the penalty area. Connelly shot smartly past Dunlop and the match was over. Even now, Everton continued to press forward and spectators were left wondering what might have happened if Burnley hadn't had that brilliant six-minute period in the first half when they took that three-goal lead.

**Burnley:** Blacklaw, Angus, Cummings, Seith, Miller, Adamson, Connelly, McIlroy, Pointer, Robson, Pilkington.
**Everton:** Dunlop, Parker, Bramwell, B. Harris, Jones, Meagan, J. Harris, Thomas, Hickson, Collins, O'Hara.

**Scorers:** Connelly (2), Pointer, Robson and Pilkington.

Adam Blacklaw.

# AFTER THE LORD MAYOR'S SHOW

**29 August 1959**
Referee: Mr M. McCoy

**Burnley 1 West Ham United 3**
Attendance: 26,783

Burnley proved yet again that they could be infuriatingly inconsistent as they plunged to defeat against West Ham. Already the detractors were saying 'here we go again' and the *Burnley Express* described the formula as 'an uncertainty which is more gloomy than glorious'. Burnley's defeat of Everton had prompted high hopes and the brilliant warm sun continued to shine on the Turf Moor faithful.

West Ham had forgone their traditional claret and blue for obvious reasons and they wore all white, with a thin claret-and-blue line round the waist. They had arrived with a blaze of publicity about their modern training methods, which included weight-lifting!

The very young Burnley team faced an inspired goalkeeper in Dwyer and he made several international-class saves. The expected threat from Hammers' centre forward Keeble was nullified by Brian Miller, but Grice made up for it, giving Tommy Cummings an afternoon he would want to forget.

Burnley v. West Ham. Pointer goes in for a challenge with Brown on the left and Bond on the right.

Bobby Seith.

Yet it seemed that the Clarets would carry on form where they left off with Everton, when John Connelly scored after only three minutes. It was not to be, however, and Woosnam was on hand with the equaliser only four minutes later. From then on West Ham took control, with Grice looking the best player on the field and the Burnley attack looking disjointed and lacking in confidence. Cummings, McIlroy and Blacklaw all had bad days as the team struggled.

The first half ended with the score even, Smyllie having missed an easy chance in front of an undefended Burnley goal. The second continued with the Hammers dominating the match and it was fully deserved when Smyllie put them ahead with a speculative shot.

Worse was to come. With Burnley struggling to find a way back and Jimmy Mac having his worst game to date, Grice gained possession out on the wing. There appeared to be no danger but Grice centred a high, floating ball which Adam Blacklaw ignored, assuming that it was floating wide. It didn't. Blacklaw, too late, flung himself despairingly across the goal but to no avail.

Burnley's man of the match, Brian Miller, tired of the inefficiency of the forward line and tried a run on goal himself, but he was easily cut out by the Londoners. Even Brian Pilkington was unable to control the ball and the match fizzled to an end with Burnley defeated. This was definitely a match for the team and fans to forget.

---

**Burnley:** Blacklaw; Angus, Cummings, Seith, Miller, Adamson; Connelly, McIlroy, Pointer, Robson, Pilkington.
**West Ham United:** Dwyer; Bond, Cartwell, Malcolm, Brown, Smith; Grice, Woosnam, Keeble, Smyllie, Musgrove.

**Scorer:** Connelly.

# DOUBLE BLUES!

**2 September 1959**         **Everton 1 Burnley 2**
Referee: Mr J.S. Pickles       Attendance: 39,000

The drought had caused severe problems in Burnley and the lack of rain had led to water rationing, but Burnley were back on Merseyside and the victims were – again – Everton. Blacklaw grabbed the headlines after his miserable time against West Ham with a superb display and such was his brilliance that the Everton fans clapped him from the pitch at the end of the match. It was Burnley's first 'double' of the new season.

The Everton supporters were expecting big things of the Blues after their 5-2 thrashing at Turf Moor. They rightly believed that the result was not a fair reflection of the play and that if Burnley's three goals in six minutes had been removed then Everton were the equal of their opponents. Burnley weren't at their best, but Angus and Blacklaw broke the hearts of the Toffeemen.

The game started with Everton making all the running and it appeared to the sweating spectators that Burnley were continuing where they had left off against West Ham, with the notable exception of John Connelly, who was giving Parker

Training at Turf moor – Seith and Miller battle it out.

a torrid time. This apart, Everton were wasting chances with Hickson, Collins and Wignall all having opportunities to put them ahead which they failed to convert.

The first goal came when Everton were awarded a corner. Wignall cracked the ball with tremendous power and Blacklaw barely had time to react before he was picking the ball out of his net. It was just reward for Everton and the goal was the presage to a period of continuous attacks on the Burnley goal. The Clarets began to look desperate and Brian Miller floored local hero Dave Hickson, much to the annoyance of the crowd. Hickson was playing to the gallery, trying to unsettle Miller, but the young Burnley player was not to be outfoxed and Hickson became more and more subdued as the match progressed.

Ray Pointer, the blond human dynamo, was well chaperoned by Jones and he appeared to be having an ineffectual evening under the Goodison lights until Adamson passed to McIlroy and Mac opened the defence with a precision pass to the centre forward. For a split second, Pointer appeared to have let the ball go too far, then he spun and shot. The ball hit the crossbar and bounced into the goal bringing Burnley level.

Shortly afterwards, Everton right-back Parker was injured and Everton reorganised. It was half-time and both sides had everything to play for. The second half found Parker still limping but substitutes were still not allowed in British football and he had no option but to continue, limping or not. It didn't seem to worry Everton, however, and Bobby Collins moved up and narrowly missed scoring when Blacklaw made an amazing save, twisting in mid-air when he appeared to have been deceived by the flight of the ball.

Miller by now had got the better of Hickson and the Everton man tried a tackle more suited to rugby, for which he received a lecture from the referee. As the game moved into its latter stages Burnley began to play the better football and Everton, for the first time, began to look anxious. Pilkington had a chance that he placed narrowly wide then Robson mis-kicked with the goal at his mercy. Instead of the ball he clouted the turf with his foot, to the great amusement of the Evertonians.

Everton had thrown everything at their opponents but Blacklaw had broken their spirit with his brilliant display and the home team resembled a boxer who

---

**Everton:** Dunlop, Parker, Sanders, King, Jones, B. Harris, J. Harris, Wignall, Hickson, Collins, O'Hara.
**Burnley:** Blacklaw, Angus, Cummings, Seith, Miller, Adamson, Connelly, McIlroy, Pointer, Robson, Pilkington.

**Scorer:** Pointer (2).

# Everton v. Burnley

Jim Furnell.

had punched himself out. It was not altogether unexpected when Adamson passed to McIlroy, received the return then slipped the ball again to the Irishman. McIlroy looked around him and saw Pilkington. The wing-man ran with the ball past a defender and centred for Pointer, who ran on and headed a beautiful goal. There was no fight left in the Merseysiders and the first double of the season had been achieved.

# NOW IT'S LONDON BLUES

**5 September 1959**
Referee: Mr R.G. Warnke

**Chelsea 4 Burnley 1**
Attendance: 36,025

This was the match that Burnley were sure to win. Chelsea had conceded six goals in their previous match against Manchester United and their defence was perceived to have more holes than a fishing net.

Many of the Chelsea players were household names, unlike the Burnley youngsters but it was a young unknown called Jimmy Greaves who caused panic amongst the Burnley defence whenever he was near the ball. He caused all sorts of confusion with a series of passes and touches, then he would run off the ball and appear in the penalty area to snap shots at the beleaguered Blacklaw.

Perhaps there was a pattern emerging when Burnley played London clubs. At West Ham, Burnley took the lead within the first few minutes before falling apart and so it was at Stamford Bridge. It was John Connelly who scored the early goal with a sharp, accurate cross shot and the future looked bright. Sadly, the defence was having a nightmare day with only Blacklaw retaining some credit as mistake followed mistake. First, Bobby Seith's error allowed Brabrook to collect the ball and deliver a pass to Livesey for the latter to score. Then Brabrook himself fired home Chelsea's second as the referee looked at his watch at the end of the first period.

Team talk at Gawthorpe led by Potts before the away match at Chelsea.

# CHELSEA v. BURNLEY

Jim Furnell.

In the second half Jimmy Greaves ran riot and he was awarded a very dubious goal when both referee and linesman appeared not to notice that he was in an offside position. Greavesy was dominating the game and Burnley's defence resembled mesmerised rabbits caught in the beam of a car headlight whenever he got the ball. The rabbits paid dearly when Greaves slotted a pass through for Livesey to score Chelsea's fourth. It was clear that there was going to be an abundance of goals scored both for and against Burnley in the rest of the season. The only question was would the Clarets score more than their opponents? The team had shown that they could beat the best. They'd also shown that on some days they could forget how to play altogether. It was going to be an interesting season. No one knew just how interesting.

---

**Chelsea:** Matthews, Sillett, Tindall, McMillan, Scott, Anderton, Brabrook, Greaves, Livesey, Tambling, Blunstone.
**Burnley:** Blacklaw, Angus, Cummings, Seith, Miller, Adamson, Connelly, McIlroy, Pointer, Robson, Pilkington.

**Scorer:** Connelly.

# WINNING WAYS AGAIN

8 September 1959                         **Burnley 2 Preston North End 1**
Referee: Mr K.A. Collinge              Attendance: 29,175

After seven games in less than three weeks it was back to winning ways, but not without countless missed chances. Preston had the mighty Tom Finney on the wing and the crunching Willie Cunningham at right-back. Cunningham was a full-back of the old iron-man mould. His bone-breaking tackles made you wince even if you were at the back of the stand and his whole demeanour was intended to put fear into the hearts of wingers – and it usually succeeded. Would he have lasted a match without a red card in modern football? Cunningham marked Pilkington's card early on and he hit the winger hard with a late tackle, leaving him prone on the turf. The Clarets were playing with energy and enthusiasm, but subtlety wasn't apparent in the early exchanges. Frustratingly for the fans, there was always one superfluous pass when a shot would have been more productive.

Preston were playing neat football and Finney, although he was being kept fairly subdued by young John Angus, was occasionally crossing with his usual accuracy. But Burnley were keeping possession and doing most of the attacking without looking very threatening. Robson snatched at a shot on the edge of the area and Pointer missed his kick when a good chance came his way. Else, in the Preston goal, saved well from Seith, then his goal was kept safe when Cunningham headed a Connelly effort away on the goal line. Adamson was next in line and his shot went just wide before North End broke away and went for goal. Taylor sent an accurate through pass to Sneddon and he saw Blacklaw advancing and cleverly chipped the 'keeper. Angus tried his best to head the ball away but to no avail. Burnley were trailing.

Preston were playing some sweet, methodical football now and they almost doubled their advantage when Sneddon lashed in a shot from twenty yards. Blacklaw was on hand and he palmed the ball away only to see it bounce towards the goal line. With the Preston fans already cheering for a goal he scrambled across the goal mouth and regained possession to keep the score at 1-0.

The Burnley forwards were not causing the Preston defence any real worry – they were shooting wide and high and even Jimmy McIlroy seemed out of sorts until he flashed past Cunningham and passed to Robson, who headed for the far corner, only to see Else make a desperate fingertip save. Burnley were doing all the attacking and chances were going begging as they insisted on embellishing with the extra touch. Preston were not only soaking up the pressure, they were making it look easy and their defence was totally in control as Burnley struggled to gain some reward for their authority.

# BURNLEY v. PRESTON NORTH END

Jimmy Robson.

On the occasions when Preston did attack they looked cool and sophisticated in comparison, with Finney chipping delightful crosses into the area and the rest of the team appearing to have all the time in the world to play their cultured game. Blacklaw had to be on his toes and he made an excellent save from Hatfield as Preston again threatened to put the game beyond Burnley's reach.

Harry Potts called for his team to throw caution to the wind and Adamson and Seith joined in the attacks, with the result that Preston's defence began to lose its composure. Shots rained in on Else's goal and were saved or charged down. Pilkington had a long, hard shot saved and Connelly's effort skimmed past the post. It was desperate stuff and the crowd were ferocious in their support of the Clarets. At the other end Preston had a corner and O'Farrell volleyed from fully thirty yards only to see his effort tipped over the crossbar by Blacklaw.

---

**Burnley:** Blacklaw, Angus, Cummings, Seith, Miller, Adamson, Connelly, McIlroy, Pointer, Robson, Pilkington.
**Preston:** Else, Cunningham, Walton, Fullam, Dunn, O'Farrell, Finney, Milne, Hatfield, Sneddon, Taylor.

**Scorers:** Pointer and Robson.

# Burnley v. Preston North End

The match had reached its last twenty minutes when John Connelly, Burnley's main danger-man, beat a couple of players and ended on the left wing, where he seemed to lose possession. He regained the ball when all seemed lost and centred hard for Pointer to slam home a header. It was attack all the way now and Pilkington had a shot saved when Else tipped the ball over the top, then from the resultant corner kick he punched clear. Pointer had a header saved and the match was heading for a draw when Connelly centred for the umpteenth time for Robson to head home. Preston girded their loins for one last mighty effort but it was too late and Burnley had taken two more points.

John Angus.

# NO CLARET DROUGHT

**12 September 1959**

Referee: Mr A. Holland

**Burnley 2 West Bromwich Albion 1**

Attendance: 23,807

---

This was the week when the water was turned off for all households in the town between 6 a.m. and 6 p.m. The drought situation was grave. Household water had been turned off and water had to be obtained in containers from stand pipes. Burnley sweltered in temperatures around the mid-seventies and after a month without rain the water stocks were at their lowest for thirty-five years.

It was also the week when the Burnley cricket professional, Collie Smith, was killed in a car crash in his early twenties. Collie Smith was a well-oved professional and he was known too for his charity work and as an ambassador of the game. He was sadly missed. At a memorial service on the pitch before the match against Rawtenstall, Rev. W. Ridyard, who had been Collie's host in Burnley, described him as a 'troubadour of God … this merry Andrew of cricket'.

There was sad news on the jobs front too, as the textile industry's death rattle echoed round the town and mills closed in ever increasing numbers. The only area, it seemed, where there was any joy was at Turf Moor football stadium. Against West Bromwich Albion, Jimmy McIlroy stole the show with a display of courage and genius. I can vividly remember Mac leaving the field with an injured shoulder and returning, heavily bandaged, and going out on the right wing with his arm strapped to his side. It's a great credit to the sportsmanship of the Albion team that they didn't play on his injury, especially as he turned the game with his brilliance.

The heat was merciless throughout the match and West Brom's Kennedy and Burnside also suffered injuries, both leaving the pitch for a short while in the first half. Connelly was again Burnley's outstanding attacker in Burnley's early play, but the heat was having an effect and the game was generally scrappy and uninspiring. The situation was not helped by the West Brom tactics, which included all manner of fouls. Referee Holland allowed many misdemeanours to go unpunished when keener control would have improved play.

Just before half-time Bobby Robson, who would later manage England, took a long shot, more in hope than expectation. Blacklaw seemed not to see it and the ball looped into the net for a disappointing half-time score of 1-0 to West Brom.

The second half was a different affair. One-armed Jimmy Mac was sending accurate and teasing centres into the box, tormenting the West Brom defenders in the torrid heat. The defence was looking good, with Brian Miller the pick of the bunch, and Blacklaw made amends with a superb save from Robson. Burnley were putting on the pressure and West Brom were wilting. It was a deserved

Alex Elder.

# BURNLEY v. WEST BROMWICH ALBION

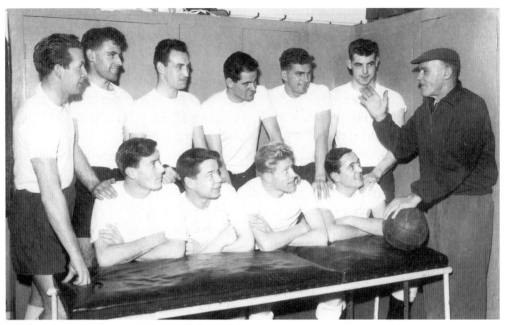

A dressing-room tactics talk from coach Ray Bennion.

equaliser when Miller brought the ball deep out of the Burnley half and passed to Connelly, who sent a delightful pass across the field to Pilkington. Pilkington centred and there was the reliable Robson – the Burnley version this time – to tuck the ball into the net: 1-1.

The game was on and Burnley continued to move forward and appeared to have taken the lead when Connelly shot home, only to have the 'goal' disallowed for offside. It was a dubious decision but justice was done within two minutes when McIlroy, one arm and all, passed accurately from the right wing to find left-winger Pilkington, who scored the winner.

It was a fine victory and showed that the young team could dig deep into their resources when fortune seemed not to favour them. Ronnie Allen, the idol of West Brom, had been neutralised. McIlroy had been injured after only ten minutes with a cynical foul and more than one Claret had the scars to show after the game.

**Burnley:** Blacklaw, Angus, Cummings, Seith, Miller, Adamson, Connelly, McIlroy, Pointer, Robson, Pilkington.
**West Bromwich Albion:** Potter, Howe, Williams, Setters, Kennedy, R. Robson, Allen, Burnside, Kevin, Jackson, Hoggs.

**Scorers:** Robson and Pilkington.

# DEEPDALE GLOOM

**15 September 1959**                    **Preston North End 1 Burnley 0**
Referee: Mr L.J. Hamer                    Attendance: 27,208

The continuity of team selection meant that regular supporters knew the team without looking or listening to the pre-match announcements. Amazingly, Burnley would play fifty matches in the season and use only eighteen players. Most small boys could rattle off the team without thinking.

Not so against Preston. Jimmy Mac was still injured and Bobby Seith had foot trouble. A young lad called Alex Elder made his debut at full-back and Tommy Cummings moved into the half-back line.

This game, although of course no one knew it at the time, signalled the beginning of Burnley's vintage period. Alex Elder was the last piece of the jigsaw and when McIlroy returned he would complete the team which would, with the notable exception of Bobby Seith, be responsible for the celebrations the following May and which many regard as the best Burnley team ever.

Alex Elder faced the most difficult debut any full-back in English football could have. He was set to mark the 'Preston Plumber' and England winger Tom Finney. Finney was acknowledged as one of the best wingers in the world at the time and still is Preston North End's greatest hero.

Elder's debut started disastrously when, after only six minutes, Taylor took a corner which seemed to be covered by John Angus. Angus, however, failed to head clear and, out of a scrummage of players, Tom Finney appeared minus his debutant marker and headed home.

Burnley pressed hard and once again Connelly looked to be the most dangerous of the raiding Clarets. He forced Else into a desperate save then he looked certain to reach a Pilkington centre when Else raced from his line too late and was relieved to see Milne save the day for Preston with a desperate challenge. Next Miller tried a crack but was off target, then Robson saw his shot parried and on the rebound he mis-timed his second attempt and the ball went high into the crowd.

Cunningham was the star of the North End defence and his long balls were reaching Finney with regular precision. Finney was expected to give young Elder a torrid time but Elder had different ideas and soon the great man was drawn into the middle to shake the young Irishman off. Sneddon replaced Finney on the wing for a while but still Elder wouldn't let Finney free.

At the other end White, Jimmy McIlroy's stand-in, drove accurately at goal but the ball bounced off Milne and bobbed safely into the hands of Else. Then Adamson split the Preston defence open with a fine pass to Pilkington and he

# Preston North End v. Burnley

centred to an unmarked Jimmy Robson but the ball spun away and the chance was gone. Burnley were in the ascendancy, but when North End broke away they looked dangerous and from one counter-attack Blacklaw was forced into a fingertip save from Lambert.

Burnley's forwards were showing their inexperience as Preston defended calmly and resolutely. The youngsters were snatching at passes in their eagerness to find the equaliser but their play was improving all the time and Adamson, Cummings and Connelly all had efforts blocked. North End were falling back and crowding their area now but Connelly was still causing them problems. Numerous offside decisions went against Burnley as Preston's experience exposed the weaknesses of youth.

White was industrious but McIlroy's generalship was sadly missed as passes went astray. Burnley played at one pace and Cunningham marked Pilkington out of the game for long periods, using both fair and foul means in roughly equal measure. Pilkington became frustrated and at one time he crunched into Cunningham with a full-blooded shoulder charge – not a wise move against the Preston hard man.

The game was becoming more and more physical and eventually Cunningham was booked for a particularly strong tackle. From the free-kick Cunningham, Dunn and O'Farrell, all from Preston, were injured in a collision! The game was held up to allow them to receive treatment, after which they all resumed play.

Pilkington was next to be booked when he fouled the Preston centre forward Alston as Burnley pushed for an equaliser. The fouls flew in thick and fast as the frantic pace increased, but the wiles and experience of the North Enders proved too much for the youth and eagerness of Burnley. Alex Elder left to an ovation from the Burnley supporters. It was the first of many.

---

**Burnley:** Blacklaw, Angus, Elder, Adamson, Cummings, Miller, Connelly, White, Pointer, Robson, Pilkington.
**Preston North End:** Else, Cunningham, Walton, Milne, Dunn, O'Farrell, Finney, Sneddon, Alston, Lambert, Taylor.

Billy Marshall.

# MAGIC FOR MAGPIES

**19 September 1959**         **Newcastle United 1 Burnley 3**
Referee: Mr R.H. Windle        Attendance: 38,570

The drought continued and Burnley worried as players complained of swollen feet after playing so many matches on rock-hard surfaces. Bobby Seith had been the first to drop out of a match, but it was feared that more would follow. For the Newcastle match, however, the players could relax in the knowledge that the pitch had been watered using water from the Tyne.

The long-suffering supporters, still complaining because Burnley had only finished seventh in the division the previous season, were already of the opinion that the team was too young and inexperienced. 'Another mid-table year' they pronounced confidently.

Not all the players were in their first flush of youth. Jimmy Adamson, Burnley's captain, was making his 300th first-team appearance. The skipper hailed from Ashington, just down the road from St James' Park Newcastle, as had many of the young Clarets. So many, in fact, that the club allowed them to stay in the Newcastle area and visit their families after the match.

Harry Potts surprised the travelling supporters by selecting Elder. Cummings moved to centre half whilst the youngster retained his full-back position.

The opening period was a torrid time for the Clarets as Newcastle powered forward, with attack following attack, prompted by the silky skills of Eastham, Allchurch and Bobby Mitchell. Veteran half-back Scoular was dominating the game from the back (as his fellow defender Bob Stokoe would do in years to come) and his scintillating passes repeatedly threw the Lancastrians on their heels. Newcastle were noted for their exciting attacking football, albeit more notably in the cup, and in the opening period they seemed set to take Burnley apart.

When Burnley began to settle down, after about twenty minutes, Adamson, and, to a lesser extent, the still far-from-fit McIlroy began to take over and create openings for Pointer and Connelly. Unfortunately, Connelly, who had been selected to play for England the following week, was injured early on and he missed two chances with only the goalkeeper to beat. It was clear that a fit Connelly would have done better. With both Connelly and McIlroy playing at half-pace, the omens weren't good for Burnley and the match wasn't an attractive spectacle.

Elder was outstanding. He took Hughes out of the game with superbly-timed tackles and astute marking and, on the other flank, the tricky Bobby Mitchell was similarly obliterated by Angus. The two young defenders showed remarkable maturity and no little talent and Newcastle supporters were reduced to hoping that Eastham would turn up trumps to provide an opening – and that is precisely what happened when Eastham ran at the defence, causing panic and confusion. First Cummings left Tait free to try and stop him, then Angus too tried a tackle, but as Eastham went down he slipped a pass to the now unmarked Tait, who opened the scoring by clipping the ball past the advancing Adam Blacklaw.

The lead galvanised the young Clarets and Burnley went straight on the attack: a free-kick from Robson found Pointer who bore down on goal. When scoring seemed a formality, Stokoe appeared and brought Pointer down in the area, but referee Windle was a long way from play and he awarded a free-kick, to the obvious disappointment of the Burnley fans and players.

The free-kick proved to be as good as a penalty. McIlroy appeared to take it but instead he jumped over the ball and Adamson lofted a pass to Pilkington. McIlroy, in the meantime, had run through the Newcastle defence which stood stock-still, looking totally bemused. Pilkington passed across the box back to Mac who slammed the ball home. Newcastle still hadn't moved.

For the rest of the half Burnley defended robustly – too robustly at times as free-kicks were given away. With the half moving to a close Eastham, by a long way the man of the match for Newcastle, dribbled the ball for a full thirty yards leaving defenders in his wake, and Blacklaw was forced to turn the ball round the post.

The second half started well. Miller broke free from deep in defence and released a pass to Pointer, who cheekily back-heeled it to Robson. Robson's shot rebounded and Connelly put Burnley ahead with a fierce first-time shot.

If the home supporters expected the usual passionate Geordie fight-back they were sadly disappointed. For once, perhaps as a result of the stultifying heat, United seemed incapable of coming back into the game. The match disintegrated into a dull affair with the wing-men blotted out and the centre of the park dominated by Cummings. Eastham continued to look dangerous, but only he and Allchurch looked to have any spirit left.

Elder nearly scored during this period with a thirty-five-yard shot which curled just wide, then at the other end the defence seemed to lose concentration as Allchurch burst through and hit the post.

---

**Newcastle United:** S. Mitchell, Keith, McMichael, Scoular, Stokoe, Bell, Hughes, Allchurch, Tait, Eastham, R. Mitchell.
**Burnley:** Blacklaw, Angus, Elder, Adamson, Cummings, Miller, Connelly, McIlroy, Pointer, Robson, Pilkington.

**Scorers:** Connelly (2) and McIlroy.

# Newcastle United v. Burnley

Burnley continued to rule the roost and Pilkington began to have an increasing influence on proceedings. The match was sealed from a corner when Connelly took a short kick to McIlroy, who returned the pass and watched as the wing-man hit a shot from an impossible angle which beat everybody and went into the net.

Newcastle were beaten, but in the final minute the tough old war horse Jimmy Scoular clattered into Alex Elder and Elder was left with a large bruise for his troubles.

Not a pretty match, but a victory at Newcastle with two players far from fit was an excellent result. Perhaps it wouldn't be a mid-table year after all.

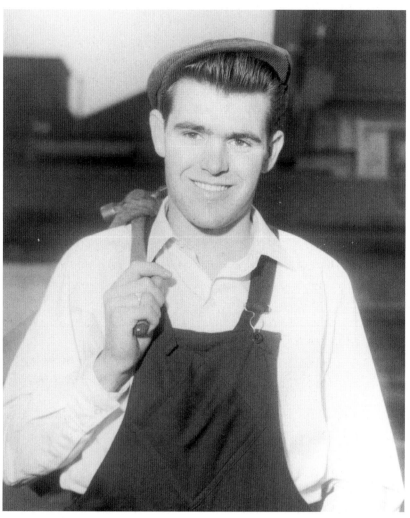

John Connelly receives news of his first England cap (against Wales) whilst at work at Bank Hall Colliery.

# BOOM BOOM BRUMMIE

**26 September 1959**
Referee: Mr J. Cook

**Burnley 3 Birmingham City 1**
Attendance: 23,471

Burnley had made their best start to a season for six years and they had twelve points from their first nine matches, so a visit from bottom club Birmingham was confidently expected to end in two points for the home side.

Gil Merrick, the suave-looking moustachioed England goalkeeper, dominated the Burnley forwards with his superb positional play, but even he could not deny Burnley victory against a woefully weak Blues team. Indeed, Burnley's play was casual such was their confidence and the Birmingham defence seemed – with the exception of their 'keeper – to be almost non-existent. The Clarets appeared at times to be amazed at the ease with which they could wander through the Birmingham defence and as a result they lost their impetus.

Jimmy Mac was still not at his best but the defence rarely looked in trouble and Alex Elder gained a standing ovation from the home crowd for the mature way in which he blotted out the opposition.

Only ten minutes passed before Pointer received a centre from Pilkington and headed home and most people expected an avalanche of goals, but Burnley seemed content to play pretty passes which went unchallenged without threatening Merrick.

Suddenly, Burnley were undone when, in a rare foray into the Clarets' half, Orritt latched on to a long ball and scored, to the disbelief of the supporters. Worse almost came a few minutes later when Orritt hit the Burnley post. After this brief threatening spell, Birmingham began to threaten in an altogether more unacceptable manner. The fairness of their tactics deteriorated and referee Cook had to speak to them on numerous occasions as the first half drew to a close.

Birmingham opened the second half on the attack and Blacklaw had to make a fine save from Larkin before Burnley finally changed up a gear as they realised that the points were not theirs by right.

McIlroy began to exert his influence on the match and Connelly started to run at the full-back. The inevitable goal came from McIlroy, who headed home a sharply-hit cross from Robson. Birmingham disintegrated completely and Burnley ran through at will, but somehow they didn't convert their dominance into a cricket score and had to wait until the last minute for McIlroy to centre for Connelly to score from close range.

It was the second successive match that Burnley had won even though they had failed to find form. Nevertheless, they had gained another two points and the obvious gap in class between them and the woefully inept Blues was there for all to see.

# Burnley v. Birmingham City

Tommy Cummings.

---

**Burnley:** Blacklaw, Angus, Elder, Adamson, Cummings, Miller, Connelly, McIlroy, Pointer, Robson, Pilkington.
**Birmingham City:** Merrick, Sissons, Farmer, Watts, Smith, Neal, Hellawell, Gordon, Larkin, Orritt, Hooper.

**Scorers:** Connelly, McIlroy and Pointer.

Bobby Seith.

# WINNING THEIR SPURS?

| | |
|---|---|
| 3 October 1959 | Tottenham Hotspur 1 Burnley 1 |
| Referee: Mr R.H. Mann | Attendance: 42,717 |

With the defeat of Birmingham, Burnley moved into fourth place in the First Division, only one point behind leaders Tottenham Hotspur. Arsenal and Wolverhampton Wanderers were second and third respectively with 14 points – the same as Burnley.

The Keirby Hotel, symbol of the brave new Burnley of the 1960s, was preparing for a March opening and was hailed as 'The Claridge's of the North'. Could the football team gain similar accolades?

The Clarets travelled to top-of-the-table Spurs without Jimmy McIlroy, who was on international duty for Northern Ireland. Spurs, for similar reasons, were without Danny Blanchflower, Dave Mackay and Goalkeeper Brown. A win could take Burnley to the top should Wolves and Arsenal fail to win.

The heatwave and drought continued and White Hart Lane was blisteringly hot for the match. It was the hottest October day on record and several people from the crowd were helped out by St John's Ambulance volunteers. One young lad from Burnley travelled to the match and gained brief fame later in the year by appearing in a photograph, handkerchief tied round his head, in (I believe) *The Football Annual for Boys*.

Spurs opened with some delightful one-touch football and Burnley were exposed as the young and inexperienced team which they were. White looked uncomfortable in this exalted company and Robson once again looked over eager. After eight minutes Spurs took the lead when Harmer flicked the ball over the defence to Smith, who passed diagonally to Medwin who shot low past Blacklaw.

Tottenham fans were pleased with progress so far and for a while their team continued to dominate. Harry Potts took a hand and ordered White and Connelly to exchange positions and immediately White began to settle down. Now Burnley were in the ascendancy and Spurs looked less composed, with Adamson and Miller taking Harmer and Dunmore in hand. With Harmer nullified Spurs lost their direction.

Smith, the stocky England centre forward, was subdued by Tommy Cummings who had a fine game, but it was Adamson who looked composed and authoritative as he stamped his personality on the match. Jones and Medwin swapped places for Spurs but to no avail and they faded from the game.

Spurs did have a chance to put the game beyond doubt when a cross hit the crossbar and was cleared by the ever improving Alex Elder.

# TOTTENHAM HOTSPUR v. BURNLEY

Ian Lawson.

**Tottenham Hotspur:** Hollowbread, Baker, Hopkins, Dodge, Norman, March, Medwin, Harmer, Smith, Dunmore, Jones.
**Burnley:** Blacklaw, Angus, Elder, Adamson, Cummings, Miller, Connelly, White, Pointer, Robson, Pilkington.

**Scorer:** Miller.

# TOTTENHAM HOTSPUR v. BURNLEY

Potts (left) watches a training session at Turf Moor before the away game at Spurs on 3 October.

Pointer and Miller came within reach of converting chances but the equaliser remained elusive. Cummings received a stern lecture for obstructing Smith, then Smith himself dived theatrically when tackled by Adamson and gained a free-kick which happily came to nothing.

Burnley piled on the pressure as the precious seconds ticked away and chances fell to Pilkington, Pointer and Connelly – but were spurned. Sixty seconds were left when Elder joined the forwards in a desperate last-ditch attempt. It was Elder who latched on to the ball and passed to Pilkington, who saw that Miller too had joined the attack. The ball went back to the big half back who, from a very tight angle, struck home the equaliser to the delight of the heat exhausted players and fans.

The match was still not over and with the last kick White had a chance to set up an unmarked Pointer for the winner but he hesitated for a fraction and the chance was gone. This was an honourable draw for the youngsters. Arsenal had lost to Everton and Wolves had slammed Luton 5-1 at Kenilworth Road, so Spurs and Wolves now had 16 points, with Burnley third on 15. The pot was boiling. No one knew just how hot it would become.

# FARMER GEORGE

**10 October 1959**                         **Burnley 1 Blackpool 4**
Referee: Mr W. Crossley              Attendance: 26,620

This was a match which Burnley expected to win but, having the infuriating knack of being wholly unpredictable, they defied the odds against a Blackpool team struggling in the lower reaches of the table and with only three wins to their credit. The performance was roundly condemned at the time, but in fact Burnley looked the better team for long spells and they met Scotland's goalkeeper George Farm in best form. Many of the fans, the author included, looked on in disbelief as he produced a string of brilliant saves. We thought at the time that it was a significant result which firmly underlined that we weren't really in the race for the League title.

The key difference between the teams was that Blackpool attacked directly and simply and Durie showed how to score goals. Burnley on the other hand played prettily, but as had happened so often in the season they added one pass too many or looked over eager. It was a disturbing trend and few people left Turf Moor believing that the team could possibly be credible title challengers.

Burnley v. Blackpool. Armfield clears away from a McIlroy attack.

# Burnley v. Blackpool

Burnley v. Blackpool. The goalie clears from Pointer and McIlroy.

It all started brilliantly, with every indication that the Seasiders would be torn apart when McIlroy passed to Connelly who hit a through ball to Robson. Robson shot but the ball rebounded and he hit it again, watching his shot beat Farm high into the net.

Blackpool equalised a few minutes later through Kaye in a rare journey into the Burnley half but even then Burnley looked totally in control, sweeping the ball round the pitch with majestic ease. There was still a feeling that they would run out easy winners – until Blacklaw was caught off his line and lobbed by Durie.

Burnley were 2-1 down and the match was still not quarter of an hour old. The two Kellys played well for the Pool, tackling hard and fairly and throwing the

---

**Burnley:** Blacklaw, Angus, Elder, Adamson, Cummings, Miller, Connelly, McIlroy Pointer, Robson, Pilkington.
**Blackpool:** Farm, Armfield, Martin, J. Kelly, Gratrix, H. Kelly, Hill, Peterson, Mudie, Durie, Kaye.

**Scorer:** Robson.

Burnley forwards off balance. Any team plan seemed to disappear and Blackpool had some dangerous breakaway raids which threatened the home goal.

The Claret fans could claim bad luck and a non-Claret referee. The second Blackpool goal should have been disallowed for offside, then Pilkington was flattened in the area for what appeared to be a penalty, only for Mr Crossley to wave play on. As the half progressed the tangerine-shirted defenders gave away ten free-kicks in quick succession and as many more fouls went unpunished.

Burnley had no fewer than nineteen corners and many were scraped away by desperate last minute hacks, rebounds off forwards and saves by the immaculate George Farm.

It was not to be. Burnley provided the pressure and Blackpool the goals, with Durie scoring two more to carry his tally to three and his team to four. It was a dispiriting result but on another day some of the shots would have gone in, penalties would have been awarded and mistakes, such as the poor pass by Angus which gave away the fourth goal, wouldn't have occurred.

Perhaps the bad game was out of the system. It was hoped so, because the next match was against arch rivals Blackburn Rovers. As a result of this defeat, Burnley slipped to fourth place, three points behind leaders Tottenham.

Jimmy McIlroy.

# CALAMITY!

17 October 1959        **Blackburn Rovers 3 Burnley 2**
Referee: Mr N.N. Hough        Attendance: 33,600

Standpipes were still being used in Burnley as the drought continued. To children it was great fun: no baths and journeys out into the street ostensibly to fill kettles with water but in reality to waste water by squirting it at friends before being told off by a conscientious adult. It was the first time that standpipes had been used since the First World War.

The Turf Moor faithful who travelled to Blackburn for the local derby cared not a jot as their team went down to the old enemy, making it two defeats by local rivals in a week and the alarming loss of seven goals.

Adam Blacklaw was not having a good run and some blamed him, unfairly, for the Blackpool defeat and compared him unfavourably with the man who was still seen as Burnley's first choice 'keeper, the injured Colin McDonald. Perhaps this had an effect on his performance at Blackburn. Whatever the reason, he was not at his best.

Burnley were without John Connelly, who had been called up to play for England and Harry Potts experimented with a curious line-up, with Pilkington playing on the right wing (I believe for the one and only time) and Gordon Harris coming in into Pilkington's usual left wing spot. Robson was replaced by Billy White.

It was later stated that this was possibly the first match to which Harry Potts committed his team to a form of 'total football' with defenders swapping positions and covering for each other as the demand arose. Possibly the system had been tried against Blackpool in the previous week's debacle. Certainly there had been much in that match which had been difficult to explain in the days when every player was supposed to stick to his position.

Alex Elder was entrusted with marking the man who would have been playing for England had it not been for Connelly's success. Bryan Douglas was the right winger who had replaced the great Stanley Matthews on the flank for England – a selection which made him in the eyes of many an imposter and charlatan. In Blackburn he was the hero, but to Elder he was just another player to be efficiently marked.

Burnley's plans were thrown awry by a touch of individual genius when, having beaten three defenders, Dougan shot home to give the lead to Rovers.

The match developed into a tough contest with tackles, fair and unfair, in abundance. Smith flattened Jimmy Mac twice and was spoken to by the referee as were Angus, Vernon, Pilkington and McLeod. Without a shadow of doubt, had

Bolton Wanderers v. Burnley. Douglas goes in aid of the fallen Elder.

the match been played twenty years later half a dozen players would have left the field.

Burnley began to dominate the fast but not very skilful match and, after Bobby Seith feigned the taking of a free-kick, Jimmy McIlroy slotted the ball to the lurking Pilkington at the far post and the tiny winger shot home the equaliser.

The apprehension being displayed by Adam Blacklaw was concerning the Burnley fans and players and within minutes Dobing fired in a shot from an acute angle which Blacklaw had covered. Sadly, the big 'keeper seemed to fumble and the ball shot off his hands, over his shoulder and into the net. It was a joyous moment for the delighted Rovers fans.

---

**Blackburn Rovers:** Leyland, Bray, Pickering, Smith, Woods, McGrath, Douglas, Dobing, Dougan, Vernon, MacLeod.
**Burnley:** Blacklaw, Angus, Elder, Seith, Adamson, Miller, Pilkington, White, Pointer, McIlroy, Harris.

**Scorers:** Pilkington and an own goal.

# BLACKBURN ROVERS *v.* BURNLEY

Rovers were in command now, but Harris and White were linking well on the left, giving hope that all was not yet lost. The first half belonged to Blackburn.

The second began with Burnley attacking fiercely and Billy White missed a chance to equalise early. Fans were bemused by the fact that Burnley's defenders were joining in the attacks. Shots rained in the direction of Leyland's goal but too often they were off target or saved by the 'keeper.

Then fate took a hand when Miller and Seith combined in attack. Miller turned a free-kick to Seith and his shot rebounded to Douglas, who had fled to defence and for once lost his Alex Elder shadow. Douglas, looking harassed and confused for all the attention he had received from the youngster, swung a scything kick in an attempt to pass back but the ball looped gently in the air over the head of Leyland for Burnley's equaliser.

Douglas looked inconsolable and had to be taken to the centre for the kick-off by Woods.

Adamson, Elder and Angus all joined in the attacks and it seemed inevitable that Burnley would grab the winner. Rovers looked to be on the ropes and a brilliant pass by Seith sent Pilkington goalward. Pilkington passed to White, White to Miller and Miller to Harris. Harris shot and the ball whistled past the post with the 'keeper well beaten.

Rovers scored the decisive goal totally against the run of play. They were awarded a free-kick near the Burnley penalty area and Vernon lobbed the ball over the wall in the vague direction of the goal. Blacklaw appeared to be put off by the advancing Douglas, but for whatever reason he totally misjudged the flight for the second time in the match. Again his error was costly and the ball looped in for the winner.

Late in the game the Clarets continued to press and they looked the better team, forcing Leyland into two excellent saves as the last minutes trickled away. A point was not to be, however, and Burnley drifted further away from the top with their second successive defeat.

One elderly fan, on leaving the ground was heard to say 'I bet when Douglas sits down for breakfast tomorrow he'll still find Elder next to him'.

# BACK TO WINNING WAYS

24 October 1959
Referee: Mr A. Hawcroft

Burnley 4 Manchester City 3
Attendance: 29,228

---

With standpipes still operative, the rains fell, making the task of walking to and fro with water containers in the street even more unpalatable. The water was eventually switched back on the following week. At Turf Moor, the floodgates opened in a different sort of way in a seven-goal thriller of a match.

The arrival of free-scoring, in-form Manchester City suggested that a deluge of goals would be the order of the day. City were in fifth position in the First Division and had won five games on the trot as well as scoring 30 goals. With Burnley's defence leaking badly in the previous two games, the stage seemed set for drama. In the previous season, many of us had witnessed City beat Burnley 4-3 on a gloriously sunny opening day of the season after Burnley had led 3-0 at half-time.

City were a cavalier, attractive team with heroes such as the great Bert Trautmann in goal. Trautmann had gained fame at Wembley in the Cup Final four years previously when he had played with a broken neck.

The fact was that both teams hit form and played open, exciting football. City looked to their maestro George Hannah and Burnley, of course, to Jimmy McIlroy. Goals were on the cards. Goals were what we got.

Burnley tore into City from the start and the light blues reeled under the pressure. Their game plan was to mark Jimmy Mac as tightly as they could and they dedicated two defenders to the task, but Mac was back to full fitness and at his mesmerising best and he left the defenders flat-footed with almost monotonous regularity. He was responsible for the first goal when he drew two defenders out of position and found Pilkington, unmarked, with a precise pass. Pilkington, without hesitation, beat Trautmann.

Similarly, goal number two was the result of McIlroy brilliance. This time he went out on the left wing, beat the hapless Sear and centred to Pointer – the centre forward making no mistake in guiding the ball into the net.

City had obviously done their homework on Blacklaw and suspected that long shots would test his confidence after the sorry Blackburn affair, but this time the 'keeper  dealt competently with the long range efforts; City changed their ploy and Barlow cracked in a point blank shot which Blacklaw saved brilliantly. The half ended with Burnley in control after an exciting, absorbing game.

The second started badly, with niggling fouls and no clear-cut chances. The referee didn't help by letting infringements go and then stopping the game for niggling offences. Elder and Angus, growing in stature with every game, were nullifying the potential threat of Barlow and Colbridge and City were reduced to

# Burnley v. Manchester City

breakaway raids in the short breaks between the almost continuous Burnley attacks.

Then there was a heart-stopping moment when Ray Pointer sprinted like a greyhound and tried to turn with the ball at high speed. He slipped and crashed head first into the wall behind the goal, the back of his head cracking into the stonework. Trainer Ray Bennion, club doctor Doctor Iven and a posse of ambulance men appeared around the stricken centre forward, who was carried off. People feared the worst and a subdued buzz ran round Turf Moor. Amazingly, the blond dynamo returned to continue some minutes later.

The match suddenly fizzed back into life, with Hannah and Mac once more finding their respective touches. Hannah started the City attack which led to their goal with a pass to Barnes, and it was Hannah himself who finished it by scoring from Barnes's return.

Burnley seemed to have the match sewn up at 2-1 but Billy White was determined to improve the 'goals for' column and he scored Burnley's third from close range, then minutes later he popped up out of a crowded area to make it 4-1.

The match seemed over now, but the Burnley fans who had witnessed the City comeback in the previous season knew that there were still twists in the tail. The plot started to corkscrew when Blacklaw began to display the edgy persona which he had adopted of late. City took heart and Hannah scored his second: 4-2.

The seconds ticked by and Colbridge at last escaped from the attention of the tiring John Angus to score City's third; now it seemed that a tide of sky blue was pouring through the Burnley defences and City must equalise and for the second year running cancel out a three-goal Burnley lead.

The whistle blew with the Clarets hammering a clearance upfield. Burnley were back on the winning trail.

When the dust settled on this match Burnley had leapfrogged City in the League and were in seventh position, just three points behind leaders Tottenham. Little did anyone realise that when these two clubs faced each other at the end of the season it would be a match of indescribable tension and excitement, with the championship as the prize.

---

**Burnley:** Blacklaw, Angus, Elder, Seith, Miller, Adamson, Connelly, McIlroy, Pointer, White, Pilkington.
**Manchester City:** Trautmann, Lewers, Sear, Cheetham, McTavish, Barnes, Barlow, Hannah, McAdam, Hayes, Colbridge.

**Scorers:** White (2), Pointer and Pilkington.

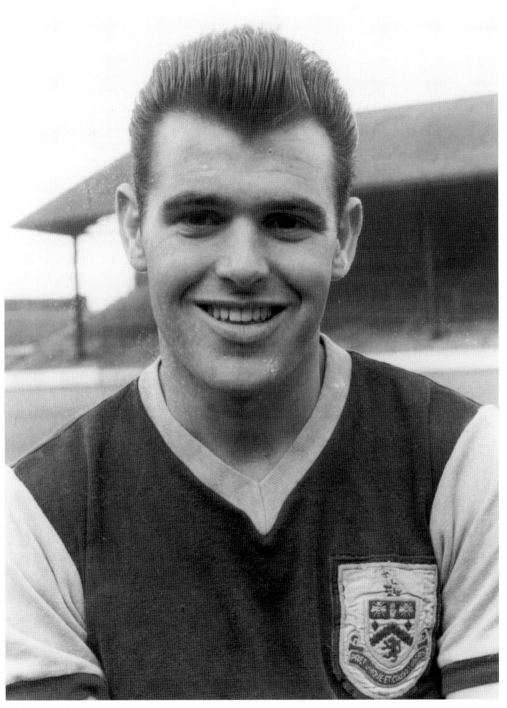

John Connelly.

# WEDDINGS AND HATTERS

**31 October 1959**              **Luton Town 1 Burnley 1**
Referee: Mr G. W. Pullen         Attendance: 15,638

Bob Lord was in trouble in the courts again. This time he was fined and ordered to pay costs when a dirty finger bandage was found in a stew supplied by his shop. Mr Lord's defence was typically abrasive but to no avail.

Burnley travelled to Luton, the losing cup finalists in the previous season. Luton were currently bottom of the table but had proved in the past to be something of a bogey team for Burnley. So it proved again in a dismal encounter.

Burnley's first half performance was almost totally without merit and, had Luton been more competent up front, then they would have led handsomely at the break. Bingham and Pacey both missed easy chances, then repeated the procedure to prove that it was not an accident the first time.

Only Jimmy McIlroy seemed at ease in this lacklustre display in which players fell over each other and became confused in their attempts to develop the new style of play. The only highlights of the first forty-five minutes were goals by Brown

Airborne attack from Pointer and Connelly.

50

Brian Miller.

after 9 minutes for Luton and an equaliser from Pointer, which he scored with a rasping shot on the turn that would have graced a much better game.

Eventually, as the match progressed, Burnley began to show some neat touches but the tiny Kenilworth Road pitch and the crowding tactics of the Luton defence proved to be too much of an obstacle.

Frankly, there was little to say about this thoroughly dull encounter. It did seem, however, that the chance of Burnley challenging for the top was very remote indeed. With less than two thirds of the season remaining, Burnley were in seventh position, four points adrift of leaders Spurs. More alarming was the goals ratio so far. Spurs had scored 36 and conceded only 17 whereas Burnley had scored 31 and conceded 29: definitely not championship form.

My day was spent in Burnley at St Peters church, where I sang in the choir at the wedding of my sister, Pat. I made a thorough nuisance at the reception at Stirk House by asking everyone if they knew how Burnley had got on.

---

**Luton Town:** Collier, Dunne, Daniel, Brown, Kelly, Groves, Bingham, Morton, Pacey, Turner, Warner.
**Burnley:** Blacklaw, Angus, Elder, Seith, Miller, Adamson, Connelly, McIlroy, Pointer, White, Pilkington.

**Scorer:** Pointer.

# WOLVES WALLOPED

7 November 1959
Referee: Mr K. Howley

Burnley 4 Wolverhampton Wanderers 1
Attendance: 28,093

Wolves, reigning champions and the current season's top scorers with 45 goals from their 15 matches, were next at Turf Moor. In their last season Wolves had scored 110 goals in 42 matches. Given the frailty of the Burnley defence most people thought a hammering was due.

A hammering it was, but the old gold shirts of Wolves were the ones on the wrong end of the scoreline as Burnley once more reserved their best performance for top-class opposition. Wolves were considered to be the best team in the land and having won the League in successive seasons they were confidently seeking a hat-trick this year.

It seemed strange to see a Wolves team without Billy Wright, the England captain, playing at centre half. Wright had recently retired. For Burnley, Robson was back, replacing Billy White.

The household names of Wolves opened well with the speedy South African Horne trying to gain the advantage on the left wing. Angus dealt effectively with him and soon the match slipped into a fascinating clash of styles, with Wolves preferring the full-blooded charge and Burnley mounting subtle raids, prompted by the in-form McIlroy. Wolves tried to crowd Mac out of the game, sending several defenders to mark him, but the Irish genius was at his best and even when surrounded by top class defenders he would leave them flat footed with a shimmy of the hips and a flash of speed before sending a perfect pass to an unmarked colleague.

Wolves were stretched and Burnley won a string of corners and free-kicks which Jimmy Mac floated tantalisingly into the area, causing the Wolves to look as if they thought that the ball might explode at any minute.

The opening phase was won handsomely by Burnley and their opponents looked shaky and indecisive. Their indecision was a major factor in the first goal, when Flowers and Stuart each waited for the other to cut out a pass. Pointer, on the other hand, did not hesitate and he latched on to Flowers' delayed back-pass and shot home for the opener.

The celebrations hadn't died down when Wolves equalised out of the blue. The kick off went directly to Flowers and he passed to Mason from the left and the inside right obliged by banging the ball in past Blacklaw.

The game was alive, with Wolves counter-attacking and Burnley still looking the better of the two teams. It was all they deserved when Connelly cracked in a hard drive and Robson flicked the ball on past Finlayson to regain the lead. The crowd was ecstatic as the champions tried to fight back, only to be thwarted by the rock-solid young defenders.

With the referee looking at his watch in readiness for half-time, Pilkington beat Flowers and burst down the left wing before centring to Pointer who made no mistake from close range, giving the unhappy Finlayson no chance. The half-time whistle blew with Burnley holding a two-goal lead after their best display of the season so far.

The second half was as quick as the first, with Wolves sticking to their attacking plan. In goal, Finlayson dominated his area and even barged his own right-back Kelly off the ball when he went for a high cross, but Burnley had a firm hold on the game and only a series of rebounds and last gasp saves prevented them from going further ahead.

Burnley v. Wolves. Sidebottom clears away a Pointer attack.

---

**Burnley:** Blacklaw, Angus, Elder, Seith, Miller, Adamson, Connelly, McIlroy, Pointer, Robson, Pilkington.
**Wolverhampton Wanderers:** Finlayson, Kelly, Harris, Clamp, Stuart, Flowers, Deeley, Mason, Murray, Broadbent, Horne.

**Scorers:** Pointer (2), Robson and Connelly.

# BURNLEY v. WOLVERHAMPTON WANDERERS

Burnley v. Wolves. Pointer just misses a diving header.

At the other end, Murray was thwarted by a fine save from Blacklaw as Wolves broke away and thoughts of the Manchester City comeback must have filtered through many minds. John Connelly tried to end all such thoughts by latching on to a McIlroy pass and scoring number four.

Even then, Wolves tried to get back but the Burnley defence was in commanding form with the backs, Angus and Elder, seemingly impassable.

As Mr Howley blew for time every Burnley fan knew that they had witnessed an exceptional performance. With their best performance of the year, Burnley moved up to fifth in the First Division, one place behind Wolves. Both teams had 20 points and above them were West Ham United on 21 and Tottenham Hotspur, surprisingly beaten at home by Bolton Wanderers. Burnley, for their part, would have to learn to beat the lesser teams if they were to mount a serious championship challenge. For the moment, however, the crowd went home savouring a fine triumph.

# FOUL OWLS!

Sheffield Wednesday were known as the 'yo-yos' because of their propensity for bouncing between the First and Second Divisions. There was, at the time, a well-known story about a Wednesday supporter who greeted the presentation of the Second Division Championship trophy with the comment 'I never want to see the bloody thing again'.

Their amazing record for the 1950s was: 1949/50 promoted to First Division, 1950/51 relegated to Second Division, 1951/52 promoted to First Division, 1954/55 relegated to Second Division, 1955/56 promoted to First Division, 1957/58 relegated to Second Division, 1958/59 Champions of Second Division and promoted.

They were aiming for mid-table respectability, but they had the worst strike rate in the division – having scored just 20 goals – and they occupied fourteenth position. Defensively, however, they had also conceded only 20 – which was ten less than the Clarets. Even more telling was the fact that they had conceded only four at Hillsborough all season. Sheffield's defence contained England goalkeeper Ron Springett and defenders on the verge of international honours, like Megson, Swan and Kay. A dour struggle was forecast.

In truth, Wednesday hit the Clarets like missiles, with tackles that often crossed over the line of law and order. Sadly, Mr Leafe was lenient.

The star at the start of the game was a black dog which invaded the pitch, holding up the game for several minutes. It may have been this incident which caused the defences to have lapses in concentration because both goals were scored within minutes. As the dog was led from the pitch, Wednesday gained possession and a long ball found Wilkinson who passed back to Ellis who headed home via the crossbar.

Burnley immediately attacked and scored the equaliser. Pilkington and McIlroy overlapped, bamboozling Megson, who attempted a weak challenge for the ball and allowed Robson to nip in. Nip in he did and he shot past the current England 'keeper for Burnley's goal.

The game settled down after this and defences dominated, with Angus and Elder once again giving notice of the great partnership that was developing. Adam Blacklaw was commanding in goal, perhaps to celebrate the fact that he'd been selected to play for Scotland under-23s – becoming the seventh Burnley player to be honoured during the season.

Burnley persisted in trying the long high ball to Ray Pointer but Swan, the

# Sheffield Wednesday v. Burnley

Wednesday centre half whose name was soon to be linked with football scandal, proved big enough to deal happily with everything in the air.

Connelly, due to play for England at Wembley the following Wednesday, was injured in a crunching Megson tackle and Fantham flattened McIlroy with an appalling charge in the back. Both players were effectively down to fifty per cent. Then Fantham charged at Blacklaw, who was in the process of tipping a shot over the bar. The big Scot swung on the crossbar and lifted his legs to allow the villainous Fantham to crash into the net. It was pantomime stuff and the hapless referee was being roundly jeered by both sets of supporters.

Although his injury was clearly hampering him, Connelly still proved dangerous and Springett made two excellent saves – the second full length from a rasping shot which seemed all the way a goal.

By this stage, both teams were tackling hard and not always fairly. Curtis was happy to foul Pilkington at will, charging in and hitting the little winger with great force. Pilkington, however, was not as soft as his baby-faced looks and stature suggested and he soon realised that he had Curtis beaten for both pace and skill and, as the match progressed, Curtis found himself on his bottom watching the back of the Burnley winger with infuriating regularity. Pilky sent over several accurate centres, one of which ended in Robson slamming the ball against the bar.

For Wednesday, Ellis was the greatest threat and his runs caused problems for the Burnley defence. After long periods of Burnley pressure, Wednesday threw caution to the wind for a final attack and it was Ellis who had the last chance and he crashed into Blacklaw as the whistle went, leaving the Burnley 'keeper prone on the turf as the game ended.

It had been a hard and brutal experience for the youngsters and they'd emerged with the claret and blue flag flying high – and proved that they could mix it with the toughest when the need arose.

---

**Sheffield Wednesday:** Springett, Curtis, Megson, McAnearney, Swan, Kay, Wilkinson, Young, Ellis, Fantham, Finney.
**Burnley:** Blacklaw, Angus, Elder, Seith, Miller, Adamson, Connelly, McIlroy, Pointer, Robson, Pilkington.

**Scorer:** Robson.

Brian Miller.

# PIECES OF EIGHT

**21 November 1959**                          **Burnley 8 Nottingham Forest 0**
Referee: Mr P. Hackney                        Attendance: 24,349

---

Following their hard-earned draw at Hillsborough, Burnley dropped to sixth position. Spurs, the leaders, moved to second after drawing with Blackburn Rovers and West Ham United went top, courtesy of a 3-1 win at Arsenal. Only two points separated the leaders from Burnley and there were only five points between the first and twelfth club.

The fact that the press had largely ignored Burnley over the years was a bone of contention with many Burnley supporters. The national papers still reported in detail on Wolves, Arsenal and Spurs but the only information generally available about the Clarets was in the results column. Harry Potts' new style of football was changing that and the drubbing of title favourites Wolves made a clear statement of intent to the football world. For the first time, the newspapers were beginning to take Burnley seriously. The young Burnley players had won international honours, almost unnoticed by anyone outside the town, and against Nottingham Forest Burnley had nine players on view who had international recognition.

In 1957 Forest had beaten a flu-depleted Burnley 7-0 and Burnley were looking for revenge. Billy Gray, an ex-Burnley stalwart, returned with Forest playing on the right wing and was given a sporting ovation as he ran on to the pitch.

Robson and Pointer had both had some stick from the demanding Burnley fans and, whereas Pointer had settled in, Robson still suffered from adverse criticism from those who felt that he hadn't the qualities needed to succeed. It was clearly affecting his play and although Harry Potts had once again shown faith, the twenty-year-old was nearing that crucial stage where he had to make his mark. A minority of fans groaned when they discovered that he had been selected, proclaiming loudly that he didn't have the necessary attributes for first team football. How wrong they were.

Like his much criticised contemporary Roger Hunt of Liverpool, Robson had the gift of being in the right place at the right time to poach goals. The fact that his control wasn't as good as that of Jimmy Mac was irrelevant.

Forest without a doubt underestimated Robson. They recognised the threat of Jimmy McIlroy and Ray Pointer and marked each of them assiduously, leaving room for Robson to wreak havoc.

There was no answer to Jimmy McIlroy. The understanding which he was developing with his young forwards and his ability to dictate the pace of the game was shown at its best and poor Forest were the unwilling victims of a virtuoso display.

# Burnley v. Nottingham Forest

At times Mac seemed to have the ball attached to his feet as he drifted and shimmied his way past the bemused defenders. Subtly weighted passes would confuse defenders and leave them flat footed, then electric bursts of speed would end with simple prods to the unmarked forwards. It was a delight to watch.

Forest, for their part, showed none of the petulant peevishness of Sheffield Wednesday. Perhaps if the had done, the scoreline would have been respectable, but to their eternal credit they played fair football to the end, even forcing Adam Blacklaw to make a couple of first-class saves and the defence to be on its mettle.

In the opening exchanges both teams played open, attacking football and Billy Gray, on his return to Turf Moor, let fly a whistling shot which Blacklaw did well to save. For a short while, Connelly and McIlroy swapped positions and the ploy immediately paid dividends when they linked together and Connelly's shot was palmed away by Thomson to Robson, who scored number one. Burnley were looking good but there was no indication of things to come.

Pilkington was next to get in on the act when he received a pass in his own half. He looked up and seeing no one in a better position he ran hard with the ball, surprising full-back Forest. No one could touch him for pace and suddenly Pilkington saw the goal and let fly with a cross shot which beat Thomson by dint of its sheer speed: 2-0.

Forest were on the rack now and they looked confused as Burnley launched yet another attack. Things went from bad to worse for the red shirts as Whare was carried off injured and Whitefoot also sustained an injury.

Forest tried to employ the offside tactic with disastrous results. Jimmy McIlroy was the arch destroyer of offside attempts with his last-second passes and swift short runs and Forest caused themselves untold problems. McIlroy weighted a pass to Adamson in midfield, Adamson sent it to Pointer, Pointer to Robson, Robson smacked it into the net: 3-0 and match over.

Even this wasn't enough, and before half-time Pointer scored a fourth and Robson scored his hat-trick and Burnley's fifth. The crowd were either ecstatic or stunned, depending on their allegiances. 5-0 at half-time!

Pointer added a sixth in the second half when he cheekily nipped in to a long ball from Angus which had dropped harmlessly, or so it seemed, in the Forest

---

**Burnley:** Blacklaw, Angus, Elder, Seith, Miller, Adamson, Connelly, McIlroy, Pointer, Robson, Pilkington.
**Nottingham Forest:** Thomson, Ware, Patrick, Whitefoot, McKinlay, Iley, Gray, Booth, Wilson, Quigley, Imlach.

**Scorers:** Robson (5), Pointer (2) and Pilkington.

# BURNLEY v. NOTTINGHAM FOREST

penalty area – Thomson's ball. Not so. With the 'keeper ready to collect it, the blond bomber appeared from nowhere and headed the ball over the goalie and into the net.

Forest were being thrashed, but their nightmare did not end there. Number seven came from hat-trick man Robson with another header. Then Forest began to attack and for a while the Burnley defence had to hang on as Gray tried to work his magic, in spite of close attention from the ever improving Elder.

There were seven minutes to go and Burnley were seven goals up when Pilkington beat his marker for the umpteenth time and centred for Pointer to end the rout. Even then the Clarets wanted more but the whistle blew. Forest disappeared as rapidly as their tired legs would carry them and Burnley received a standing ovation.

In the exhilaration of the eight goals it went almost unnoticed that the defence had kept a clean sheet for the first time in the season. Jimmy Robson's haul of five goals was a post-war record and Burnley moved into fourth position, still two points behind leaders West Ham. What Billy Gray thought as he left the pitch is unrecorded. One can imagine.

Burnley v. Nottingham Forest on a murky night at Turf Moor.

# MATCH OF THE GREY

**28 November 1959**
Referee: Mr W. Clements

**Fulham 1 Burnley 0**
Attendance: 29,582

It was inevitable. After the Forest game expectations were impossibly high. Championship talk was around town and there was a confidence which just a few weeks previously after the Blackpool defeat was unimaginable.

Fulham had some household names on the team sheet. International goalkeeper Macedo, Johnny 'Brylcreem Boy' Haynes, Jimmy 'Match of the Day' Hill and George '1966 World Cup' Cohen. A certain Alan Mullery was also there.

Burnley dominated the first half. Had the score at the interval been similar to the 5-0 lead of the previous match it wouldn't have been an unfair reflection of the play. Macedo made a truly brilliant save from Connelly early on when the crowd had already risen for the goal. Then the Claret forwards spurned chance upon chance from near range and afar. Every single Burnley forward missed an easy chance and the Lancastrians danced round their London opponents, making the likes of Hill, Haynes and Mullery look very ordinary indeed. McIlroy shone like a beacon.

Fulham, for all their reputation of fair and attractive football, were playing a tough game. Hill flattened Adamson and a wit in the crowd yelled 'Get Brian (Miller) to climb up his chin!' It didn't help Adamson, who was carried off. Next, Legget charged like a bull at Blacklaw. Too late he noticed that Blacklaw was standing his ground and – like many to follow – Legget found himself hurtling into a man mountain and was dumped, dazed and bemused on the floor for his troubles.

Burnley's pressure was almost total and Fulham rarely journeyed out of their half. The crowd sensed that when Burnley scored an avalanche of goals would follow, but the whole ground was stunned when Fulham, in their only attack, found Hill, who attempted a vague sort of header which looped over Blacklaw and dropped into the Burnley goal. It was injustice on a massive scale – worthy of Fulham's favourite director, comic Tommy Trinder whose opening line when he came on stage was always 'You lucky people'.

Fulham revived somewhat for the second half and it was Blacklaw's turn to steal some of the limelight appropriated by Tony Macedo when he made a remarkable save from Hill.

But a just result was not to be. It was claimed in the local London press that it was the best game at Fulham for years and the crowd clapped the players from the field. The result meant that Fulham overtook Burnley, who dropped to sixth position, four points behind new leaders Preston North End.

# Fulham *v.* Burnley

Jimmy Adamson.

---

**Fulham:** Macedo, Cohen, Langley, Mullery, Lampe, Lowe, Key, Hill, Leggat, Haynes, Chamberlain.
**Burnley:** Blacklaw, Angus, Elder, Seith, Miller, Adamson, Connelly, McIlroy, Pointer, Robson, Pilkington.

# FULHAM v. BURNLEY

Jimmy Hill, the Fulham inside right was also the spokesman for the players' union and he was instrumental in bringing about the end of the fixed contracts and maximum wage structure for players. In 1959, players often signed up for a club when they were seventeen years old and once they had put pen to paper they were effectively tied to the club for the rest of their careers, unless the club decided to make a profit by selling them. They were also subject to a nationally agreed maximum wage of about £20 a week. Hill's Burnley opposite number eight, Jimmy McIlroy, had spoken out to the Junior Chamber of Commerce in Burnley. He described the contract system as being fifty years out of date and proposed that players should sign contracts of three years or less and renegotiate them when the time came. He went on to say 'If I were earning, say, £40 a week this season I would have to play the best possible football to get the same contract … next season.'

Jimmy believed that the changes, already operating abroad, would come about but not in his playing career. He also suggested that some young players who found it difficult to get into the first team should be loaned to clubs such as Accrington Stanley or Bury, who would be responsible for paying the wages during the loan period. Finally, he criticised the European Cup, saying that football was becoming secondary to winning at all costs.

But back to Craven Cottage and the Fulham robbery. There were those who said that Burnley flattered to deceive. The Forest game, they claimed, was proof. Even if their prognosis was correct, this was truly a match that Burnley should have won and won well against an experienced and accomplished team.

John Connelly.

# BYE BYE BASHERS

**5 December 1959**  **Burnley 4 Bolton Wanderers 0**
Referee: Mr A. Murdoch  Attendance: 25,706

The last month of the decade saw Burnley beat a Bolton team which had acquired the unfortunate but accurate nickname of the 'Bolton Bashers' and with their victory, although in sixth place, they were within three points of leaders Preston North End.

The super-fit Bolton team tackled ferociously, but the first quarter of the match was closely contested with both teams playing attractive, attacking football. The Wanderers relied heavily on their wingers, but Angus and Elder nullified this tactic and the Clarets' subtlety and ability to change their pace, style and tactics began to have an effect as time wore on.

Yet again Burnley were facing an international 'keeper – in this instance Eddie Hopkinson – and Hoppy's form, combined with the hard-tackling, harrying style of his defence, kept the Clarets in check until a Connelly shot came back off the inside of the post and Pointer was on hand to score with a header from the rebound.

From then on the Bolton defence grew increasingly lawless and ruthless in their tactics and by the time the second half was underway Hartle had been warned after a foul on Pointer. Burnley responded encouragingly by ignoring the challenges and scoring their second. McIlroy had drifted to the wing and when he gathered the ball and centred Bolton discovered, too late, that Connelly had moved into the centre. They watched aghast as he calmly prodded the ball into the net.

Hartle continued his policy of man or ball and a general mêlée occurred when he flattened Pilkington. Pointer was next to be laid out, along with the corner flag, as Burnley continued on the ascendancy and Bolton continued to plumb the depths.

Bolton at last moved into gear and Parry and Stevens supported their outstanding player, Hill, as they tried to find a way back into the game. Hill missed a sitter then had a shot saved by Blacklaw before Burnley regained control.

The Clarets mounted a series of attacks. They were looking dangerous and after a number of shots which were blocked or saved, Pointer and Robson went near with powerful volleys before McIlroy picked up a rebound and banged the ball into the net to sew the match up. Mac was brilliant and he was marked by no fewer than three defenders now, which left enormous gaps for the other forwards to exploit.

# BURNLEY v. BOLTON WANDERERS

Bolton were beaten long before the final goal came when Jimmy McIlroy was brought down by goalkeeper Hopkinson with a rugby tackle. McIlroy himself took the penalty. He had missed two penalties on the trot in international matches for Northern Ireland, so he desperately needed to score to avoid the disgrace of an unenviable hat-trick. He had previously developed a style of kick in which he kidded the goalkeeper into going the wrong way. Not this time. He simply strode up and slammed the ball hard into the net: 4-0.

Twenty goals in the last four home matches. Three points behind the League leaders and real proof that the Burnley youngsters could more than hold their own when the going got tough. Burnley fans were expecting a happy Christmas.

Burnley v. Bolton Wanderers. Robson fires in front of Stanley.

---

**Burnley:** Blacklaw, Angus, Elder, Seith, Miller, Adamson, Connelly, McIlroy, Pointer, Robson, Pilkington.
**Bolton Wanderers:** Hopkinson, Hartle, Farrimond, Stanley, Higgins, M. Edwards, Birch, Hill, Stevens, Parry, Holden.

**Scorers:** Pointer, Connelly, McIlroy (2, 1 penalty).

# GUNNERS OUTGUNNED

**12 December 1959**  
Referee: Mr A.W. Sparling

**Arsenal 2 Burnley 4**  
Attendance: 26,249

The Christmas season was coming and the people of Burnley prepared. They could spend their hard-earned money on a box of Christmas crackers 3s 6d, Christmas cake 9s 6d, a box of Milk Tray 2s 9d, coffee, half a crown a tin. Alternatively, a bottle of French wine would set you back 7s 3d and twelve pints of Massey's best beer would get you drunk for a guinea. A four pound chicken cost 14s 3d and half a pound of red salmon 3s 6d.

Over the festive season, Burnley visited Highbury, a bogey ground for them, and Bobby Seith played his 200th match for the Clarets. Poor Bobby was transferred later in the season and to the club's discredit they didn't present him with a Championship medal – a deed which was rectified forty years later when he received his medal in an emotional ceremony at Turf Moor.

Burnley hadn't scored at Highbury since the 1955/56 season and the press were there in force waiting to see another Burnley failure against the big guns. Highbury was, and still is, an intimidating place for visiting teams. In those days, entering what were referred to as the marble halls was similar to visiting a stately home and many teams were beaten before they even reached the pitch.

The youngsters of Burnley were unimpressed by the gentlemans' club air of the surroundings. It was to be yet another astounding win for Burnley in this astounding season. Burnley were unchanged – yet again. The team seemed to pick itself and injuries were rare. They also faced yet *another* international goalkeeper – this time Jack Kelsey of Wales. Away form had been giving cause for concern – a win had last been recorded on 19 September.

The stark facts of the match were that Burnley were 2-0 at half-time and a limping Jimmy McIlroy seemed to be pretty well out of things. He suffered a badly bruised groin for which would return to haunt him later.

All seemed lost, but Burnley outplayed the Gunners in the second half and gave one of their best displays – ever. In other games West Ham had been 6-2 by Blackburn Rovers and Spurs and Preston had both drawn. This meant that Burnley moved into third position, two points behind leaders Preston. Talk of the Championship began to circulate again.

The mixture of youth and experience was beginning to establish itself as a formidable footballing force, with players such as Pointer, Connelly, Robson, Miller, Angus and Elder linking smoothly with the experienced Adamson, McIlroy and Seith.

Burnley played in white shirts with claret numbers and from the start they were thrown by the push-and-run tactics of the Gunners who excelled in backing up. Arsenal played a patient, waiting game, pushing the ball around until an opening became available. The game was progressing as an absorbing contest until disaster struck.

Jimmy McIlroy stretched to send Robson clear with a pass, but he crashed to the turf and doubled up in agony. Bennion, the Burnley trainer, rushed on to the pitch and treated Mac for some time but eventually Burnley's genius playmaker was led from the pitch. When he returned to play he was obviously in great pain and within minutes he was lying on the pitch again after trying to keep the ball in play.

Bad went to worse when Haverty tried a speculative, harmless-looking shot and Blacklaw let the ball slip through his hands. He could only watch, horror stricken, as it went in off the post. Minutes later the game seemed over when Jimmy Adamson fouled Clapton. The free-kick was a curious, illegal affair. Henderson had jumped over the ball and he ran at the wall like a charging bull, knocking players to the left and right of him. In the meantime, Bloomfield shot over the defenders and the ball entered the net with Blacklaw unsighted.

The Burnley players were expecting the referee to rule that the kick was illegal but, to their horror and the amazement of players and supporters alike, the referee signalled a goal. The players were outraged but the referee ignored their protests. For most teams the game would have been over. For the Clarets the game started when the whistle blew to recommence after the half-time break.

Harry Potts, the architect of Burnley's success, surprised Arsenal by ignoring convention. In those days before substitutions were allowed, injured players were placed out of harm's way on the wing. Potts decided to place the injured Mac in midfield, where to the amazement of both teams he performed brilliantly, linking with Jimmy Adamson to set up attack after Burnley attack. Mac was amazing. Once, in a moment of momentous cheek, he stood in front of Groves with the ball stationary at his feet. He grinned and lifted his foot over the ball while the amazed Groves looked on, baffled. Then McIlroy pushed the ball through the Arsenal man's legs to Pilkington, who hared off down the wing. It was outrageous and audacious.

---

**Arsenal:** Kelsey, Willis, McCullough, Groves, Dodgin, Ward, Clapton, Barnwell, Henderson, Bloomfield, Haverty.
**Burnley:** Blacklaw, Angus, Elder, Seith, Miller, Adamson, Connelly, McIlroy, Pointer, Robson, Pilkington.

**Scorers:** Connelly (3) and Adamson (penalty).

# ARSENAL v. BURNLEY

Young Brian Miller too was having the game of his life, running at the Arsenal defence as if Burnley held a comfortable lead rather than suffering from a two-goal deficit. It was a strong run from his own half which led to the Burnley opener. Miller cut in with the ball and directed a pass towards Robson, which was deflected for a corner by Wills. Miller stayed in the penalty area for the corner and when the centre came over it was he who found the ball at his feet and he was faced with the simple task of converting into the empty goal – simple that is until Kelsey grabbed the half-back's foot, foiling his goal attempt.

Penalty to Burnley. In today's game Kelsey would undoubtedly have been sent off but it was decided by Mr Sparling that he would stay. McIlroy, the usual penalty specialist, was deemed unfit to take it and after asking Angus, who declined, Adamson took it himself. The captain took a ridiculously long walk back then ran in at a jogging pace before hitting the ball to the 'keeper's left. The ball went under Kelsey and Burnley were back in the game.

Now the Clarets took Arsenal by storm. The nickname 'Gunners' should have applied not to Arsenal but to their talented opponents. Before long the scores were equal when Adamson and Miller joined the forward line. Adamson passed to Connelly and the England wing man obliged by beating Kelsey for the equaliser. It was Burnley's 50th League goal of the season.

Arsenal looked shell-shocked. Their defence became unsure and jittery as Burnley piled on the pressure, with wingers Connelly and Pilkington causing all sorts of problems. The move which led to the third goal was a delight. Pointer gathered the ball halfway into Arsenal territory and he slipped it back to Connelly, who sliced the defence open with a cross-pitch pass to Pilkington. The little winger beat the full-back with a quick pass to Pointer, who had covered an amazing amount of ground and was now on the left wing. Pointer centred for Robson, who headed the ball back to Connelly.

Connelly bundled himself and the ball into the back of the net and for the first time Burnley led. Arsenal displayed a total lack of appetite for the game. It was like watching a demolition as they backed off and Burnley took them apart.

Pointer again caused mayhem when he moved out on the right wing. He seemed in truth to be everywhere and it was from the right that he ignored a half-hearted challenge by Wills and centred to Connelly, who gleefully completed his hat-trick.

Even with a 4-2 lead Burnley didn't rest on their laurels. Wave after wave of attacks left Arsenal reeling and it could easily have ended in a rout.

For Connelly it was a 12-minute hat-trick and Burnley had proved that they could beat anyone – even with an injured Jimmy Mac. Even television was mentioning Burnley now and on the radio a commentator suggested that Burnley might even be League Champions – in a few years.

Jimmy McIlroy.

# WOE

**19 December 1959**                              **Burnley 0 Leeds United 1**
Referee: Mr C.H. Sant                          Attendance: 17,398

Leeds, one of the teams who would be relegated at the end of the season, were next to the bottom of the First Division; Burnley were third and riding high. Appalling weather – high winds and mud – and the absence of the injured Jimmy McIlroy combined to equalise the teams but it didn't explain the shock result.

Perhaps the Clarets were too erratic to be talked about as Championship contenders after all. It was the first time that the team had failed to score at home and the only consolation was that the crowd was relatively small as a result of the weather and, no doubt, Christmas shopping.

The two schemers, McIlroy for Burnley and Don Revie for Leeds, were both missing, but for Burnley it was a similar story to the Fulham game inasmuch as the chances were there for the game to be sewn up by half-time but they were spurned. The Clarets paid dearly.

Leeds were poor in the first half and wayward passing was not helped by an inability to be constructive. Burnley missed several chances, notably by Pointer, Robson, Pilkington and White, but gradually their ineptness gave Leeds comfort and confidence.

Jack Charlton was a rock in the Leeds United defence and Burnley played into his hands – or rather onto his head – by lofting numerous high ball into the penalty area for him to despatch. White and Robson were disappointing and poor Pointer was a lonely one-man attack.

The Leeds goal arrived when Cush passed to Meek and Meek, betraying his name, pushed Elder over and was delighted to realise that the referee had not seen the incident. Meek continued with the ball then centred for Overfield to shoot home.

Pointer and, to a lesser extent, Connelly tried to rouse Burnley, but Charlton and the Leeds defence had decided by now that the Burnley forward line wasn't as threatening as they had been led to believe and they were resolute in defending their advantage. Indeed, in the latter stages of the game Leeds began, for the first time, to string some attacks together and it was a disappointed crowd who greeted the final whistle.

Other results in the First Division favoured Burnley. Leaders Preston slipped to second place after an amazing 5-4 defeat at Deepdale by Chelsea. West Ham too were beaten and Burnley were in fourth place, one point behind Wolverhampton Wanderers, champions for the past two seasons, and three points behind leaders Tottenham Hotspur.

# BURNLEY *v.* LEEDS UNITED

Burnley v. Leeds. the goalkeeper collects at the feet of Robson.

Jim Furnell.

**Burnley:** Blacklaw, Angus, Elder, Seith, Miller, Adamson, Connelly, White, Pointer, Robson, Pilkington.
**Leeds United:** Burgin, Caldwell, Hair, Cush, Charlton, Gibson, Meek, Cameron, McCole, Crowe, Overfield.

# CHRISTMAS TREAT

**26 December 1959**
Referee: Mr L.I. Tirebuck

**Manchester United 1 Burnley 2**
Attendance: 62,376

Two games over Christmas, both against Manchester United. What more could a team want? Four points from two wins, that's what.

A mighty crowd of over 62,000 braved the weather for their Christmas treat, hoping to see two of the most stylish teams of English football provide a mouth-watering feast of skill. Far from being the fast-flowing football associated with these two sides, the game was peppered with nearly forty fouls on a grey, damp afternoon. The Old Trafford pitch was a mass of mud and as the game progressed it cut up badly, causing football to be a casualty. Still, the Clarets ended up with two more points.

United were the better of the two teams in the opening exchanges and switched the ball from wing to wing with some aplomb in the difficult conditions. Several free-kicks were given away as defenders tried to stay upright on the mud.

A certain young man by the name of Bobby Charlton had been recalled to the United first team following a spell in the reserves and he was causing trouble for Burnley on the left of the pitch – the second Charlton brother to give Burnley problems after the efforts of Jack for Leeds United a week before.

Burnley were having great difficulty in coming to terms with the conditions – passes were forever sticking in the mud and some of the players looked out of touch. After about twenty minutes, however, the young team, sorely missing the subtleties of McIlroy, began to settle to the task.

The dual threats posed by Charlton and the blond pin-up boy Quixall were gradually extinguished and both started to look anxious and spray inaccurate passes over the field as Adamson, Miller and Seith gained a stronghold. The pattern of play began to change.

Burnley took a deserved lead when Robson sent a long diagonal pass to Connelly and he centred. Robson had covered the ground in anticipation of the return and he beat Pointer and Lawson to the ball and scored from close range. Burnley were looking good and, within a minute of the restart, Pilkington beat the defence and crossed to Ian Lawson, who headed just over.

A feature of Burnley's play of late had been the strong runs by the athletic big Brian Miller, who would gather the ball in his own half and run at the defence, often causing fear and panic. Such was the case today and Brian mesmerised the defence, who collectively acted like a rabbit in the glare of an oncoming car's headlights. He ended in the penalty area and slipped the ball through a jumble of muddy legs for Lawson, who took the ball to the line then screwed it back from

# MANCHESTER UNITED *v.* BURNLEY

Ray Pointer.

**Manchester United:** Gaskell, Foulkes, Carolan, Goodwin, Cope, Brennan, Dawson, Quixall, Viollet, Charlton, Scanlon.
**Burnley:** Blacklaw, Angus, Elder, Seith, Miller, Adamson, Connelly, Lawson, Pointer, Robson, Pilkington.

**Scorers:** Robson and Lawson.

# Manchester United v. Burnley

Ray Pointer.

a fine angle to score number two. United were a sorry, mud caked sight and at this stage they looked well beaten.

The second half started with the mud winning the battle against football but after a while United began to look as good as we knew they could be and they started to use the wings, which were the driest part of the field. Burnley began desperate defending, conceding several corner kicks. Blacklaw was injured, then the Clarets gave away four quick corners and Charlton hit the post.

It was Charlton again who forced a cracking fingertip save from Blacklaw as Manchester United piled on the pressure but even he could do nothing when Quixall received a pass from Scanlon and scored from close in.

With a draw in their sights Manchester United piled on the pressure and Burnley defended in depth. The longer the game went on the more Burnley looked secure but even so the whistle was greeted with a mixture of relief and celebration by the loyal Burnley following.

Could this be the start of a Christmas double? There were some close studies of the league table in the *Pink* that week.

# NO DOUBLE

**28 December 1959**
Referee: Mr T. Reynolds

**Burnley 1 Manchester United 4**
Attendance: 47,253

No. A double wasn't coming. If ever the season was typified by two results… Mac was back and hopes were high. Sadly it was clear from the outset that Mac was not fit, or anywhere near fit, and United blocked him out of the game, which in turn starved the forwards of the service to which they were accustomed.

Burnley flattered to deceive and their play at times looked pretty and entertaining but once in front of goal they looked and were ineffective against a well-organised United defence. Pointer, as usual, covered immense amounts of ground but at times he resembled the fabled headless chicken and the support he needed from his colleagues wasn't forthcoming.

Having said that, Burnley played well and, had the forward line been sharper, the result might have been different. Both wingers, Pilkington and Connelly, looked dangerous in the first part of the match but they faded quickly.

Manchester United were still riding on the crest of a wave of emotion following the Munich air crash, which had decimated their team during the previous year. They were still an experimental embryonic side and Matt Busby was looking for

The Burnley crowd hope for a double over Manchester United.

# BURNLEY v. MANCHESTER UNITED

the missing links which would make the Reds the most feared team in Europe within a few years. Teams coming to Old Trafford were engulfed by waves of emotion from the terraces. It was the most difficult of venues to visit, but here at Turf Moor the expectations were different.

Early on, Burnley looked to have taken the lead when Pilkington squared to Pointer who hooked the ball into the net, but the centre forward was adjudged offside and within minutes Manchester went ahead when Charlton passed to Viollet who shot home.

Burnley pressed and it was no surprise when Pilkington centred for Robson to head a beautiful equaliser. In the next attack Burnley came within an ace of taking the lead when a blistering drive from Robson was tipped over by Gaskell, who followed this up with superb saves from Miller, then from Elder. Burnley fell behind in the second half after looking the better of the two teams for long spells, Viollet heading home.

The Clarets tried for the all important goal and Gaskell was superb, dominating his area and making three crucial saves. Then Pilkington had the goal at his mercy but he made a total hash of his chance and United had escaped. Burnley threw caution to the wind and everyone went on attack – and of course Manchester United, after defending solidly, broke away and twice they scored through Scanlon.

It was a result which bore no reflection on the play and one which Burnley hardly deserved, especially in the season of goodwill.

Would this be the beginning of the slide down the League? Home defeats against Leeds and Manchester United had caused doubts to emerge and the old hands were already writing to the newspapers saying that Burnley needed someone at the helm to eradicate their erratic performances. The worrying thing, they claimed, was that Turf Moor had long been a fortress and suddenly the team looked vulnerable on their home ground. Time would tell.

---

**Burnley:** Blacklaw, Angus, Elder, Seith, Miller, Adamson, Connelly, McIlroy, Pointer, Robson, Pilkington.
**Manchester United:** Gaskell, Foulkes, Carolan, Goodwin, Cope, Brennan, Dawson, Quixall, Viollet, Charlton, Scanlon.

**Scorer:** Robson.

# HAMMERED!

**2 January 1960**
Referee: Mr K. Stokes

**West Ham United 2 Burnley 5**
Attendance: 26,000

The new decade opened with floods in recently drought-stricken Burnley, but the Clarets needed a flood of goals to regain their dented confidence. Turf Moor, so long an almost impregnable fortress, had become a theatre of nerves for the young team and perhaps they were glad that their first fixture of the 1960s was away from home. They were still third in the table (with the other top teams also stuttering) when they faced West Ham at Upton Park. West Ham had been the First Division leaders for some time, although they had slipped from the top of late, so a tight game was forecast with both teams needing to register a win to stay in contention.

The Hammers had beaten Burnley at Turf Moor in the second game of the season and were looking for a double. It was confidently forecast by many that Colin McDonald, the Burnley and England goalkeeper who had lost his place through injury, would be ready soon to reclaim his place. He played in his first competitive game for the 'A' team against Manchester United at the Gawthorpe training ground in front of a large crowd. It was his first game since March 1959, when he had broken his leg whilst representing the Football League. Pneumonia had set in and Mac had been sidelined ever since.

First impressions were that Mac's comeback was going to plan as he kept a clean sheet against United 'A'. Sadly, it was a false dawn. He never made it back to the first team and the man who had been called the 'best goalkeeper in the world' by a leading soccer magazine of the day had, to all intents and purposes, ended his footballing career.

The Boleyn Ground was a mud bath. It was the sort of surface which inevitably caused problems for the Clarets and no one expected any semblance of skilful football. To confirm this prediction, Jimmy McIlroy was still absent due to injury.

But that pitch! Undoubtedly the game wouldn't have taken place today. There didn't appear to be a blade of grass anywhere and the drizzly rain spattered into pure mud on a thoroughly dismal London day. Burnley decided from the word go that the only way to play was to use the wings, where there was at least a semblance of firmness. This, it transpired, was an inspired decision as Pilkington had the game of his life, giving Kirkup as uncomfortable a ninety minutes as he probably experienced in his whole career.

Angus and Elder, now established as two of the most accomplished backs in the business, stopped the West Ham wingers in their tracks with a brilliant display of tightly controlled defending which belied their youth and inexperience. The

# WEST HAM UNITED v. BURNLEY

topsy-turvy season continued on its roller coaster ride.

The Clarets opened their account with an opportunist goal by Ian Lawson, who slid through the mud to score then went off – to have the mud wiped from his eyes!

West Ham, completely outplayed, equalised out of the blue when Woosnam hit a long hard shot and saw Blacklaw slip and fall, then try to save with his boot. He failed and the score was one apiece. It was a common story for Burnley and Harry Potts admitted after the match that it was a fault which needed sorting.

There followed the Hammers' only period of dominance and Woosnam had a brace of chances to give them an undeserved lead before Pilkington latched onto the ball in his own half and set off at a gallop, leaving the defenders stretching and gasping in his muddy backwash. He finally evaded a tackle and, seeing Dwyer approaching off his line, he lobbed the ball over the goalkeeper with the calmness of a park game and Burnley were in the lead. It was one of the best goals of the season.

The half progressed with Burnley growing in stature and Lawson was proving an able substitute for McIlroy. He emphasised the point by jinking the ball round a couple of defenders and passing to Connelly, who scored number three just before the interval.

The second half was viewed through an eerie twilight, the Upton Park lights being totally inadequate for penetrating the stygian gloom. Had the headless figure of Anne Boleyn walked across the ground which bore her name it would have been hardly surprising.

Burnley ignored the ghostly surroundings and continued to revel in the mud. They appeared to have scored when Adamson netted directly from a free-kick. Strange scenes followed. The referee, who claimed he had not indicated a free-kick, ruled that the goal was disallowed. It was one of a series of mystifying decisions – perhaps it was a lack of illumination in more senses than one.

Burnley continued to press and their fourth goal arrived when Seith fed a perfect pass to Miller and the big half-back sent a high ball to the wing where Pilkington, the smallest player on the pitch, rose majestically above a defender and headed the ball into the penalty area to Lawson, who turned quickly and scored.

---

**West Ham United**: Dwyer, Kirkup, Cantwell, Malcolm, Brown, Smith, Grice, Woosnam, Obeney, Dick, Musgrove.
**Burnley**: Blacklaw, Angus, Elder, Seith, Miller, Adamson, Connelly, Lawson, Pointer, Robson, Pilkington.

**Scorers:** Connelly (2), Lawson (2) and Pilkington.

Jimmy Robson.

# West Ham United v. Burnley

It was West Ham's turn to up the pressure now. With nothing to lose the Londoners swept forward and Obeney was brought down by Miller in the area. The referee waved play on in spite of vociferous complaints by the Hammers. Even the Burnley fans felt that a penalty would have been just but the myopic Mr Stokes didn't. Normally one of the best referees in the land, he was having a nightmare.

His muddy hell continued when he awarded a free-kick to West Ham after Brown had rugby tackled Burnley's Lawson. Players of both sides stood back in disbelief and the fans howled in disbelief but more was to come. The free-kick was floated in the area and suddenly the referee was gesticulating towards the penalty spot. West Ham had a penalty, but no one, not even the West Ham players, knew why. There was a suspicion that the referee was rectifying the earlier mistake but whatever Mr Stokes' reasons, Cantwell scored from the spot and the game was alive again. This time it was Burnley's turn to complain.

Burnley defended in depth – given the state of the playing surface 'in depth' was an appropriate description in more ways than one – and West Ham's revival fizzled out and the Lancastrians grasped the game by the scruff of the neck again. West Ham fell back and the referee appeared to lose control as he abandoned the ten yards rule for the numerous Burnley corners.

Pilkington was causing havoc on the left and now West Ham tried to rely on the offside rule to gain some respite from the Burnley bombardment, but such was the superiority of the visitors that there could only be one winner. The Hammers were hammered into their own muddy ground when, in the last minute, Blacklaw cleared a long ball from his area and Connelly, spotting the slowness of the tired defence, took possession of the ball. With no apparent danger to the West Ham goal he lashed in a hard, wickedly swerving shot which comprehensively beat Dwyer.

Burnley now had scored 60 goals, accrued 31 points and were second in the table. Spurs still led on 34 points on a day which saw Manchester United beaten 7-3 at Newcastle, Wolves held in a 4-4 draw at Arsenal and Preston, second before the game, beaten 4-0 by West Brom.

The season was hotting up and Burnley had shown that they could perform on poor surfaces. It was an important moment in the battle for the Championship.

# SNOW TIME FOR THE BLUES

**16 January 1960**                        **Burnley 2 Chelsea 1**
Referee: Mr R.T.E. Langdale               Attendance: 21,990

---

The new town shopping centre at St James's Street was taking shape as snow fell on Burnley, causing chaos on the roads, and a smaller than average crowd braved the cold to watch Burnley entertain Chelsea at Turf Moor – mindful of the fact that they had been on the wrong end of a 4-1 thrashing at Stamford Bridge early in the season.

Soft snow covered the surface at Turf Moor and underfoot conditions were treacherous: not encouraging when the visitors were the hard men from Stamford Bridge. An icy wind blew across the ground as the teams lined up for this key match. McIlroy was absent from the Burnley line-up.

The surface caused plenty of problems for both teams but tough tackling was to the fore. Chelsea lived up to their hard image and, regardless of the obvious danger, they hit both man and ball. Poor Ian Lawson, deputising again for the injured Mac, was floored by a pile driver of a clearance and he swayed in and out of the match, receiving treatment several times. More seriously, Pilkington had to be carried off after injuring his leg.

Crowther and J. Sillett incurred the wrath of the referee and in later years would certainly have been sent off. The fact was that they remained on the pitch to the displeasure of the crowd and the Burnley players.

In spite of having an England goalkeeper and several household names, Chelsea were languishing in the bottom half of the table and impartial observers must have wondered why the team relied so much on crude tackles when players capable of great things littered the team. On this day, however, two of the household names, Peter Brabrook and Frank Blunstone on the Chelsea wings, were dominated by Angus and Elder, who had been recognised by the *Chronicle* as the best pair of full-backs in the English game. Elder nearly scored his first goal when a long, hard drive was parried by England 'keeper Reg Matthews only for the ball to spin haphazardly towards the goal line. Matthews showed his credentials by leaping backwards and saving at the second attempt.

Elder's full-back partner, John Angus, laid on the opening goal with a perfectly placed free-kick to Robson, who scored from close range.

The conditions were taking their toll and both sets of players were slipping and falling, but still Chelsea lunged in with hard, uncompromising tackles. In the second half Chelsea came back into the game when the Burnley defence failed to turn on the ice and Blacklaw was caught way out of his goal. Peter Brabrook slipped a pass to Brooks, who stabbed in the equaliser.

# Burnley v. Chelsea

Burnley v. Chelsea.

Mistake followed mistake and just after the hour Ian Lawson collapsed in pain but the referee allowed play to continue to Burnley's advantage. Pointer, most unsuited to the surface, sliced a ball through to Robson and the ball was in the back of the net before Matthews had time to blink.

Pilkington came more and more into the game in spite of his injury and his attitude of running in a straight line to goal caused Chelsea problems which they often dealt with unfairly. Pilky paid for his skills with an X-ray on his leg after the match which showed severe swelling and bruising at the front of the leg and the ankle.

---

**Burnley:** Blacklaw, Angus, Elder, Seith, Miller, Adamson, Connelly, Lawson, Pointer, Robson, Pilkington.
**Chelsea:** Matthews, J. Sillett, P. Sillett, Anderton, Scott, Crowther, Brabrook, Brooks, Livesey, Greaves, Blunstone.

**Scorer:** Robson (2).

But Burnley had won. Other teams involved in the Championship tussle did well too, leaders Spurs beating Arsenal, and Wolves beating Manchester City. Only Preston, equal on points with Burnley before the match, slipped up by losing at home to Newcastle United. Burnley remained in second position, three points behind Spurs.

The fans knew now that the team was capable of a serious challenge. On their day they could beat anyone in the League.

Some of the players are feeling the cold!

# BAGGED DOWN AT THE BAGGIES

**23 January 1960**
Referee: Mr J.W. Hunt

**West Bromwich Albion 0 Burnley 0**
Attendance: 23,400

The go-ahead was given in this week for the Burnley Inner Ring Road. The town was changing forever and looking forward to a bright new future.

Burnley Football Club hoped to share in the brave new world, but they faced West Bromwich Albion at the Hawthorns in the knowledge that this was a bit of a bogey ground for them. The Baggies were a good footballing team so an entertaining contest was forecast. For Burnley, still unbeaten in the new decade, both Pilkington and McIlroy were on the injured list and Ian Lawson and Gordon Harris were the replacements.

Colin McDonald had been promoted and was playing in goal for the Reserves against West Brom Reserves.

West Brom fielded a very experienced team and Burnley, without their schemer McIlroy and the volatile match-winning Pilkington were probably the underdogs. It was a very young Burnley team and the ground was heavy after snow and rain – ideal conditions for the experienced Midlanders.

Burnley sorely missed the experience of the two injured stars and the situation further deteriorated when Ray Pointer was injured in a tackle with Howe and spent the rest of the match limping.

West Brom were on the prowl and shooting at will as the Burnley defence soaked up the pressure, but Albion were not creating real chances, the wingers were subdued by Angus and Elder and eventually, in the second half, Ronnie Allen, the darling of West Brom, moved out on to the left wing to attack Elder – but still to no avail.

Burnley began to come out of their defensive shell and suddenly the Baggies were on their heels, literally in the case of goalkeeper Wallace who dived the wrong way and saved a Seith header with – his heel. Lawson almost scored when he flashed in a hard drive which was saved one-handed, then Robson forced a save.

The match swung again and the balance of power returned to the home side but in truth it was a bit of a nothing game. The important thing for Burnley was that the defence held out as West Brom piled on the pressure in the latter stages of the game and it was a point well won against a skilled and experienced team.

After the match Jimmy Robson, who was celebrating his twenty-first birthday, was presented with a cake festooned with twenty-one candles.

At the top of the First Division Spurs had extended their lead by beating Manchester United, whilst Wolves won at Blackburn. The top three were: Spurs

Colin McDonald with his broken leg in plaster.

38 points, Burnley on 34 and Wolves, still chasing a hat-trick of Championships, 33. The surprise result of the day was at bottom club Luton, who beat high-riding 4-1.

---

**West Bromwich Albion:** Wallace, Howe, Williams, Drury, Kennedy, Robson, Jackson, Burnside, Allen, Kevan, Hogg.
**Burnley:** Blacklaw, Angus, Elder, Seith, Miller, Adamson, Connelly, Lawson, Pointer, Robson, Harris.

# West Bromwich Albion v. Burnley

The maestro – Jimmy McIlroy.

# TWO FOR JOY

**6 February 1960**
Referee: Mr J.H. Hemingway

**Burnley 2 Newcastle United 1**
Attendance: 26,998

My schoolboy notes on this game are interspersed with comments about the Diana Dors serialisation in the *News of the World*. I was old enough to want to read more but I was at a loss to understand why the bedroom in the famous star's house had a two way mirror through which her guests could be spied upon. Oh happy, happy days of my naïve youth.

In the same week, the Spanish Travel Bureau was advertising a fifteen day all-inclusive holiday on the Costa Brava for £24 5s.

At Turf Moor, the Magpies followed the Swans as Newcastle came to town. Newcastle were midway in the First Division but United, more noted for their dashing Cup exploits in the 1950s, were always an attractive fixture. This was no exception, so much so that the crowd stood and cheered the players off.

Newcastle had some elegant players who were well-known to the public in Allchurch, Eastham and Stokoe. They also had the hard, well respected Jimmy Scoular prowling round in defence. Curiously, Burnley faced another Allchurch brother, making it a hat-trick of matches against teams with a player from the same family.

This was Ray Pointer's day. The blond striker had been stuck without a goal for eight matches and to make matters worse his tally for the season so far was 13, providing much talk of superstition. He faced Bob Stokoe, a formidable opponent and superb reader of the game, but Pointer gave the usually imperturbable Stokoe a run-around.

Adamson too was a recruit from the North East and it was he who sent Robson – yet another ex-Geordie – away on the halfway line with a subtly weighted short pass. Robson ran forward with the ball then unleashed a tremendous drive from thirty yards to leave Harvey groping at thin air.

Ian Lawson, playing in place of the injured McIlroy, was only a part-time player as his full-time job was with the army, but he linked brilliantly with Robson and the two inside forwards ensured that Mac's absence wasn't noticed, even though the visitors provided two inside forwards, Eastham and Allchurch, who amply displayed the importance of the 'key position' as Stan Matthews called it.

It was these two who created the equaliser and it was the second delightful goal of the match. Eastham took the ball from his own half and Burnley dropped back as he approached the goal, awaiting the shot. It never happened. Eastham had spotted Allchurch unmarked and a lovely pass enabled the Welshman to net the equaliser.

# Burnley v. Newcastle United

Both teams were playing attractive exciting football, notwithstanding hard tackles being made by Scoular and Miller. Allchurch and Eastham were still causing all sorts of problems and another Magpie goal seemed inevitable when Miller hopelessly mis-kicked the ball and Scott found the goal at his mercy from a few feet out. Perhaps Scott was more surprised than anyone because he missed the chance. Blacklaw saved well from Allchurch and Scott but Pointer was looking more dangerous by the minute and he and Lawson worked well for the winner. Lawson slotted a through ball to Pointer on the right and Pointer shimmied right and headed for goal. Harvey spotted the danger and advanced from his line to narrow Pointer's angle but the centre forward behaved with remarkable coolness and he stopped, looked up, judged the trajectory and lobbed

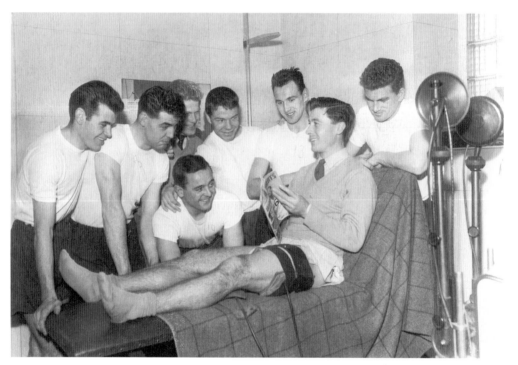

Treatment for the injured McIlroy ...

---

**Burnley:** Blacklaw, Angus, Elder, Seith, Miller, Adamson, Connelly, Lawson, Pointer, Robson, Pilkington.
**Newcastle United:** Harvey, Keith, McMichael, Scoular, Stokoe, Bell, Hughes, Eastham, Scott, Allchurch, Luke.

**Scorers:** Robson and Pointer.

... as he gets a visit from the team.

a pin-point bombshell over the 'keeper's head and into the net.

Three superb goals, a double over the Magpies, a match played in the finest spirit – even Jimmy Scoular had enjoyed a banter with both players and crowd – and two valuable points for Burnley.

It was many happy returns for the North East. Both Burnley scorers were recruited from the area. Ray Pointer had in fact matured in Newcastle junior football. The victory moved second-placed Burnley to within three points of leaders Tottenham Hotspur, who drew at Preston. Wolves drew at home to Blackpool and lay two points behind Burnley in third position. The League hotpot was bubbling nicely.

# THE BURNDEN BURDEN

**27 February 1960**                    **Bolton Wanderers 2 Burnley 1**
Referee: Mr K. Howley                   Attendance: 28,772

Burnley visited Bolton Wanderers at Burnden Park in their first League match for three weeks. It was a disappointing day for the Clarets and their defeat, coupled with a four-goal scoring spree by Spurs at Blackburn, meant that they were slipping away from the leaders. They had 36 points, five points behind Spurs and three behind Wolves. Burnley had a game in hand over both teams but with only two points for a win their task was formidable.

It was Burnley's first defeat of the year and they had both Robson and Seith absent, causing a reshuffle. Tommy Cummings returned at centre half, Adamson wore the number 4 (replacing Seith at right half) and Miller started at left half wearing what was to become his familiar number 6. Ian Lawson replaced Jimmy Robson.

The match started in disastrous fashion for Burnley when the defence was involved in a complete mix up in the third minute and Birch took the opportunity to prod the ball into the net via a defender's boot.

Burnley were impressive in their response, running the Bolton defence to a standstill and promising an avalanche of goals. Sadly, the only score was within seven minutes of Bolton's opener when a Jimmy McIlroy shot rebounded to John Connelly who converted from close range.

The Clarets were in supreme form and McIlroy and Adamson were working a partnership that was beautiful to watch – but the promised goals never arrived and when Jimmy Adamson had to receive treatment for an injury he came back limping and was never quite the same force.

Bolton's successful policy was to break out of defence and shoot on sight and the match was reminiscent of the defeat at home to Blackpool. In spite of being outplayed for long periods Bolton had two 'goals' disallowed and they hit a post. Birch was outstanding for the Wanderers and so was Holden, who seemed to be everywhere, hassling, prompting and generally controlling his area of the pitch.

For Burnley it was one of those days, perhaps caused after the excitement of the cup, when some players had off days. Adam Blacklaw seemed uneasy and jittery in goal and the usually dependable Elder was making mistakes at the back. Bolton's usual 'boot the ball or the man' tactics had an impact on the game – Adamson was brilliant until injured and Pilkington too suffered after being belted hard by Hartle, who added to Burnley's woes when he scored the decisive goal after a free-kick was awarded to Bolton on the half way line. Hartle tried a speculative lob into the area and Blacklaw was deceived by the flight. The big Scot

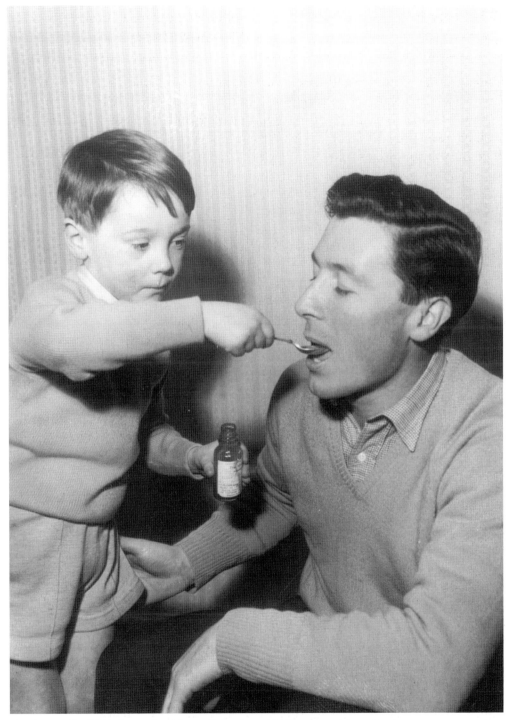

'Get better, Dad.' McIlroy takes his medicine from his five-year-old son Paul.

# BOLTON WANDERERS v. BURNLEY

Burnley v. Bolton Wanderers. Blacklaw safely gathers in front of Stevens and Miller.

took a pace forward, realised too late his error and back pedalled to try and tip the ball over the bar only to see it drop behind him into the net.

Burnley were galvanised into action but all they had to show was a chance for Connelly which he hit over the bar.

The fans who had made the short journey to Burnden Park were asked by reporters for their impressions and many thought that the championship dream was over. The less pessimistic pointed to the fact that the next match was at home to League leaders Tottenham Hotspur.

---

**Bolton Wanderers:** Bollands, Hartle, Farrimond, Hennin, Higgins, Stanley, Birch, Deakin, Stevens, Hill, Holden.
**Burnley:** Blacklaw, Angus, Elder, Adamson, Cummings, Miller, Connelly, McIlroy, Pointer, Lawson, Pilkington.

**Scorer:** Connelly.

# BLUNTED SPURS

**1 March 1960**                                    Burnley 2 Tottenham Hotspur 0
Referee: Mr D.H. Howell                         Attendance: 32,995

Tottenham Hotspur came to Turf Moor as League leaders knowing that if they beat Burnley the challenge from the Lancashire club would be effectively over. Spurs were developing into a formidable force and Danny Blanchflower predicted a 2-0 win for Spurs before the match.

The clashes between Burnley and Spurs in the early 1960s promoted everything that was good about British football. Subtlety, vision and flair were always on display and the country was glued to their sets when the matches were televised. No one could foresee it in the 33,000 crowd but we were witnessing the start of an era for both clubs.

The first half belonged to the League leaders under the Turf Moor floodlights. That is not to say that they had everything their own way but between them the elegant Blanchflower, Norman and hard man McKay ruled the centre of the pitch and set Spurs up to attack the Burnley goal. Fortunately, Blacklaw showed none of the hesitancy which had dogged him at Burnden Park when he made excellent saves, first from Allen then from Jones.

Spurs were noted for their purposeful, attacking football and many teams in this season had been beaten by half-time, shell-shocked into submission. Burnley, however, had a master tactician in manager Harry Potts and he tried different ploys to bring about a change in the direction of the game, moving Pointer was moved from centre forward to the wing and, when Spurs began to deal with that situation, back again to centre forward.

Those two great friends and Irish team mates McIlroy and Blanchflower had been absent due to international call-up at the first clash between the teams at White Hart Lane, but this time they sparred with each other, Blanchflower shadowing Mac and blocking his usual contribution. With McIlroy subdued, Burnley were second best and Jones missed a chance from ten yards when he should have given Spurs the lead. Then England centre forward Bobby Smith shot into the side netting and the Burnley supporters feared the worst.

Subtly the game began to change. Tottenham hadn't gained the early breakthrough which they had hoped for and Burnley were beginning to find a rhythm, and with it the confidence began to grow. Robson began to look sharper and his header was saved brilliantly by goalkeeper Brown and within seconds Brian Miller had a long range crack which came agonisingly close as both teams played hard, tough and fast football. Both Henry and Norman were spoken to by the referee as was Burnley's Pilkington, following which Pilkington himself was the

# BURNLEY v. TOTTENHAM HOTSPUR

recipient of a foul by Baker, who also received a short lecture. But for all of the hard stuff it was an enthralling, skilful match and Burnley, realising that a draw would be a bad result in terms of their Championship challenge, began to apply pressure in numbers with the full-backs joining the fray and moving into the Spurs area.

Harmer was exerting increasing influence on the game and nearly scored when he was thwarted by a timely Blacklaw intervention. The signs were there and the fuse was lit when Adamson and McIlroy linked to provide a through ball to Connelly who ran on and centred for Pointer to place a header between Brown and Baker for the opener. The crowd went mad and Spurs, hitherto so confident and cocksure, realised that they had a game on.

Everyone expected a fightback from Spurs and a fightback they got. Jones' shot was saved by Blacklaw and Spurs brought everyone into attack surrounding the Burnley area in a sea of white shirts – leaving themselves exposed at the rear. Burnley joyfully took advantage and when a Spurs attack broke down McIlroy gained possession and passed to Connelly and the number 7 whipped past Baker like a rocket and smashed a hard low shot past the diving Brown: 2-0.

Spurs were the ones to look disjointed now and Burnley pressed for number three and nearly scored when Brown fumbled a ball – then Spurs attacked and might have had a penalty as they stepped up the pressure for a final onslaught. But Burnley were cock-a-hoop now and they looked confident and composed, unlike their opponents who were, although dangerous, looking increasingly desperate.

The final whistle was greeted with a mighty cheer and the dark Tuesday night sky echoed to a sound which was welcoming in a team which was coming of age. The two points gained from the victory found Burnley in third position, three points behind Spurs and one behind Wolves. Crucially, they still had a game in hand over both teams.

Note: The attendance for this match against the League leaders was around 20,000 less than against Third Division Bradford City in the Cup.

---

**Burnley:** Blacklaw, Angus, Elder, Adamson, Cummings, Miller, Connelly, McIlroy, Pointer, Robson, Pilkington.
**Tottenham Hotspur:** Brown, Baker, Henry, Blanchflower, Norman, McKay, Medwin, Harmer, Smith, Allen, Jones.

**Scorers:** Pointer and Connelly.

Billy White.

# SWEET REVENGE!

**5 March 1960**                           **Burnley 1 Blackburn Rovers 0**
Referee: Mr A.E. Ellis                      Attendance: 32,281

---

It had been less than five months since Burnley had suffered successive defeats to Blackpool and Blackburn Rovers. The pundits then had written off the chances of the young team lifting the Championship and, in truth, the town's thoughts were still on the glamour of the cup and many fans would have happily exchanged two points in the League for a win against the same team, Blackburn Rovers, the following week in the quarter-final. The enormity of the moment didn't seem to strike the town until the game at Maine Road on the fateful evening in May. Back in 1960, the FA Cup was looked upon as the greatest club knockout competition in the world. British teams had only entered the European Cup in the late 1950s and it was seen as a sort of secondary event.

The game against archrivals Blackburn was viewed by many as a rehearsal, such was the importance of the cup. Indeed, it seemed that even the players wanted to reserve their best efforts for the following week and it was a dismal affair to watch. The two points gained by Burnley were going to be crucial in their League efforts but of course nobody knew that.

There is little to be written about what was probably the worst match of the season, but once again Alex Elder showed an England star – Bryan Douglas on

Burnley v. Blackburn Rovers. Rovers are down and out after Robson scores the only goal.

# BURNLEY v. BLACKBURN ROVERS

Burnley v. Blackburn Rovers. This time Leyland saves from Robson on the line. Whelan (left) watches Woods by the post.

Blackburn's right wing – that he was already one of the best defenders in the land. Douglas was moved away from the wing in an attempt to shake off the future international.

The highlight for the Burnley faithful was the headed goal by Robson from a first half corner kick. The low light was the inability of the Clarets to defeat the Blackburn offside trap and the referee was called upon with monotonous regularity to use his whistle for this particular infringement.

The 32,000 who paid to watch must have felt cheated, but at the end of the season maybe they pondered on the repercussions had Blackburn gained a point. Certainly there were some who felt that the ends justified the means and when the dust settled the simple facts were that Spurs had won and Wolves lost. Burnley's win over Rovers lifted them into second place.

---

**Burnley:** Blacklaw, Angus, Elder, Seith, Miller, Adamson, Connelly, McIlroy, Pointer, Robson, Pilkington.
**Blackburn Rovers:** Leyland, Bray, Whelan, Clayton, Woods, McGrath, Douglas, Dobing, Dougan, Thomas, McLeod.

**Scorer:** Robson.

# BACK AGAIN

19 March 1960
Referee: Mr L. Howarth

Burnley 3 Arsenal 2
Attendance: 20,166

The fans were about to participate in a crazy roller coaster ride – a mixture of brilliance, mad results and a magnificent climax on the last game of the season. Until then, the nerves and hearts of fans and players alike would be tested to the limit.

The victory over Arsenal was significant for three reasons. Firstly it proved that the young team could bounce back after the bitter disappointment of elimination from the FA Cup; secondly, an inspired decision by Harry Potts saw Adamson move into the middle as centre half and Miller to left half, (Seith, for the time being, continued at right half) and finally, the two points moved the Clarets to within striking distance of the Championship – Spurs had drawn and Wolves had been beaten. Burnley completed the trio of clubs at the top which had begun to open a gap between themselves and the rest of the division. The top three places were occupied by Tottenham Hotspur on 46 points from 34 games, Wolves in second place with 43 points from 34 and then Burnley, with two games in hand and on 42 points. The season was boiling up to a magnificent climax.

Burnley were aiming for a double over the Arsenal and it was disappointing that the reaction by the supporters to the cup defeat meant that only 20,000 fans turned up for this attractive and important fixture. Jimmy Mac was injured again and Lawson replaced him only after the army gave him permission to play. It was fortunate that they did because one of Ian Lawson's best displays in claret and blue and his pass to Pointer led to goal number one. Lawson held the ball on the edge of the area in a manner reminiscent of McIlroy himself, then, as a defender lunged in, he flicked the ball back and Pointer ran on and clipped the ball quickly past Welsh international keeper Jack Kelsey: 1-0.

Burnley were playing well and threatened the Gunners' goal on numerous occasions. Arsenal, in contrast, were trying long balls and shoot-on-sight tactics but their finishing was wayward until the Clarets delivered them a second half goal courtesy of confusion between defenders. As Adamson, Elder and Seith looked on, Henderson accepted the gift and it was one apiece.

Now Burnley got down to business. It was almost as if the preceding minutes had been a mere rehearsal. Their second goal was a tribute to the strength and tenacity of Brian Miller, enjoying his new role and assisting with the attacks. Connelly took a corner and Miller forced his way through a ruck of players and met the ball perfectly with his forehead to force the ball home.

There was only one team in it as Burnley dominated proceedings, with Ian Lawson playing a pivotal role and John Connelly mesmerising the Arsenal

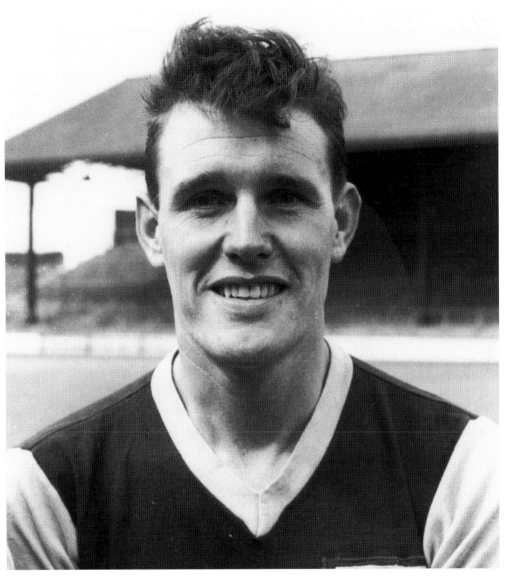

Ian Lawson.

---

**Burnley:** Blacklaw, Angus, Elder, Seith, Adamson, Miller, Connelly, Lawson, Pointer, Robson, Pilkington.
**Arsenal:** Kelsey, Magill, McCullough, Ward, Dodgin, Groves, Henderson, Herd, Clapton, Barnwell, Haverty.

**Scorers:** Pointer, Miller and Connelly.

# BURNLEY v. ARSENAL

Furnell and Marshall.

defenders with a series of incisive runs. Connelly himself sealed the match with one of the goals which were becoming his trademark. He gained control on the wing, beat the full-back and ran diagonally with the ball before unleashing an unstoppable shot past the despairing Kelsey.

In spite of their domination, Burnley lost concentration and allowed Arsenal to gain brief hope of salvaging a point. With a few minutes remaining a Henderson shot reduced the arrears and a nervous crowd must have wondered if a 3-3 repeat of the Blackburn revival was about to occur. As it was, the defence stood firm and Arsenal were offered no more chances.

# WOUNDED BY WOLVES

**30 March 1960**
Referee: Mr C.N. Rogers

**W'hampton Wanderers 6 Burnley 1**
Attendance: 38,000

---

Yet another postponement to the match against Wolves who were still in the FA Cup, meant that Burnley had a blank Saturday on 26 March. The hastily rearranged match took place on the following Wednesday and Wolves shattered Burnley. Wolves, aiming for their third League title in succession, were known as a fast playing, dashing team who tried to take their opponents by storm. For Burnley it was more of a hurricane and the team didn't have an answer on the night.

Until Burnley's defeat in the FA Cup, both Wolves and Burnley had been aiming for a League and cup double and after this game Wolves must have felt confident of achieving it. Their opponents for the FA Cup final, Blackburn Rovers, must have feared the worst.

Even when Wolves led 6-1 they still attacked, hoping to break the spirit of the Burnley team for the rest of the season by piling further humiliation upon them.

The match was summed up by a supporter who stated that 'Burnley were pretty. Wolves scored goals.'

For almost quarter of an hour the game was in the balance with Burnley giving as good as they got, then Wolves broke out of defence and Murray converted. A few seconds later and it was two when Peter Broadbent broke through on the left and centred high for Mannion to head home. Still the action continued and barely another minute had gone when Pointer signalled a false dawn by beating Slater to the Connelly centre and snapping the ball home. Two more minutes and Horne scored: four goals in five minutes!

With nine minutes to go until half-time Broadbent, always a thorn in Burnley's side, scored Wolves' fourth and the contest was effectively over. Wolves wanted more blood and Cummings (twice) and Elder saved on the goal line with Adam Blacklaw beaten.

Mannion and Mason added numbers five and six and Burnley returned to Lancashire beaten and for the present humiliated, but hopefully unbowed. For many supporters it seemed that the Championship dream had gone the same way as the FA Cup, but in fact Burnley were still four points behind the leaders Spurs and three behind Wolves – and they had those all-important two games in hand over both their rivals.

The future lay firmly in the hands of Harry Potts, who had somehow to rebuild the confidence of the shattered youngsters for the final run-in. After the Molineux debacle, however, few thought he would be able to bring about a revival.

# Wolverhampton Wanderers v. Burnley

Gordon Harris.

**Wolverhampton Wanderers:** Sidebottom, Showell, Harris, Clamp, Slater, Flowers, Mannion, Mason, Murray, Broadbent, Horne.
**Burnley:** Blacklaw, Cummings, Elder, Seith, Miller, Adamson, Connelly, McIlroy, Pointer, Robson, Pilkington.

**Scorer:** Pointer.

# FIGHTING BACK

**2 April 1960**
Referee: Mr H.N. Hough

**Burnley 3 Sheffield Wednesday 3**
Attendance: 23,123

Burnley were up against one of the League's toughest sides. A good result was essential and this time it was the Clarets who fought back from a seemingly impossible position courtesy of a strange penalty. At one time, Burnley were 3-1 down and had conceded seventeen goals in less than five games.

Sheffield Wednesday – the Owls – started where the Wolves had left off and they were one-up after three minutes when Ellis powered home. Adamson immediately reverted to centre half, swapping the left half berth with Miller, but Sheffield's style completely upset Burnley's play and Kay in particular was a very rough and tough thorn in Burnley's side, upending players unceremoniously in a continuous series of fouls. Craig too was careless with the rules and he experienced the unusual penalty of being booked.

The first half ended with Wednesday leading by a solitary goal, with the only light at the end of the tunnel being Miller's improvement at left half.

Burnley changed tactics after the break and, unusually for them, they

Burnley v. Sheffield Wednesday. Connelly (centre by post) wheels away after scoring his goal in a 3-3 draw. The goalkeeper is on the floor.

# BURNLEY v. SHEFFIELD WEDNESDAY

Burnley v. Sheffield Wednesday. Pilkington is on the left and Pointer is on the right in this goalmouth scramble.

employed the long ball, which caused the Owls some concern and led to an equaliser by John Connelly with yet another of his diagonal runs at goal. The crowd erupted, as much with relief as anything, but within seconds Wednesday were back in front when Finney headed a lob home.

Burnley's attempts to rule the game looked to be gradually coming to fruition, but just when they seemed to have weathered everything that Wednesday could throw at them disaster struck. Bobby Seith lost control and possession and the ball ran to Craig who reacted quickly and shot home.

Burnley refused to panic – a tremendous achievement after their last few games – and they were rewarded when Pointer broke free, only to be flattened in the

---

**Burnley:** Blacklaw, Angus, Elder, Seith, Adamson, Miller, Connelly, McIlroy, Pointer, Robson, Pilkington.
**Sheffield Wednesday:** Springett, Johnson, Megson, McAnearney, Swan, Kay, Wilkinson, Craig, Ellis, Fantham, Finney.

**Scorers:** Miller, Connelly and McIlroy.

penalty area. McIlroy took the result-ant kick and goalkeeper Ron Springett had obviously heard of the Irishman's penalty tricks. Mac had outpsyched the England international 'keeper, who simply stood rooted to the spot, not making any attempt to move as Mac rolled the ball gently home. Burnley were back in with a chance.

The minutes were ticking away and Burnley launched themselves for-ward, leaving themselves dangerously exposed. It was do-or-die stuff as a defeat would surely spell the end of their Championship hopes and, with two minutes to go, the bustling Miller charged out of defence and connected with the ball in the penalty area to score a dramatic last-gasp point saver.

To prove themselves as Champion-ship contenders Burnley really should have won, but it was a desperately relieved cheer that greeted the final whistle. A point kept them in the race.

Could this be the turning point? Elsewhere, Wolves beat Leeds United at Leeds by three goals to confirm their position as favourites for a League and cup double. After the Sheffield Wednesday match Burnley were four points behind both Wolves and Spurs, who were surprisingly faltering and were held at White Hart Lane to a draw by bottom club Luton Town.

Tommy Cummings.

# NO EIGHTSOME

**9 April 1960**
Referee: Major C.H. Dennis

**Nottingham Forest 0 Burnley 1**
Attendance: 24,509

The Keirby Hotel, Burnley's modern flagship building which dominated the town centre, opened for business as Burnley travelled to Nottingham. The opening was hailed as the beginning of a new era for the town.

But at Turf Moor, Bobby Seith had asked to be put on the transfer list. It was a very unpleasant saga and at the end of the season the club made the peevish decision not to award Seith with a Championship medal. It was one of Burnley's least honourable moments, rectified some forty years later when Bobby received a tremendous ovation at Turf Moor and received his medal to become one of a tiny band of players to win championships in both England and Scotland. Burnley had beaten lowly Forest by eight goals to nil at Turf Moor and now they desperately needed to complete the double to keep in touch with the Championship race.

There were debuts at Nottingham for Marshall and Meredith, who replaced the injured Elder and Connelly – the latter was playing in an international match for England against Scotland.

From left to right, back row: Cummings, Miller, Elder, Blacklaw, Seith, Angus. Front row: Connelly, McIlroy, Adamson, Pointer, Robson, Pilkington.

Brian Pilkington.

# Nottingham Forest v. Burnley

A strong, swirling and gusty wind allied to a grass-less, bumpy and dry pitch caused both teams problems. The conditions were against the Clarets more than their opponents, who were struggling at the wrong end of the division.

The ex-Turf Moor favourite, right winger Billy Gray, showed that he still had a lot to offer and Marshall had a hard time trying to subdue him, but to his credit he stuck at the task and the threat was nullified. In fact, both newcomers gave good accounts and generally the defence, led by a commanding Tommy Cummings, played well. The chances that did arise for Forest were cases of mistakes caused by the conditions and the young Clarets stayed in control throughout the match.

Jimmy McIlroy, who should have been one of those most affected by the conditions, was the star of the game, holding up the ball and mesmerising the Reds. It was Mac, on the hour, who gathered a throw in and hesitated, shuffled, then turned with lightning speed to leave Burkitt and Iley in his wake. Before the defenders had time to recover he looped a curling centre which was met by Pointer running in at his usual full pelt. Thomson was beaten and Burnley were a goal ahead. Only one team was going to win now and Pointer was denied a second when a rasping shot was turned round for a corner, then Meredith received a pass from Miller in the dying seconds and looked certain to score when the ball bobbled, causing him to shoot over the bar.

Forest had tried to cause panic with breakaway attacks through their wing men, Gray and Imlach, but Marshall and Angus were in total control and there were never any serious threats to Blacklaw's goal.

The match was a poor advertisement for soccer as the conditions and nerves on both sides combined to produce a stop-start affair, but for Burnley the points were all important in their chase for the title.

Burnley were now fourth. Spurs stayed on top despite losing at Everton, Wolves were playing in the FA Cup semi-final and Sheffield Wednesday, ahead of Burnley on goal difference, beat Leeds. But significantly, Burnley now had two games in hand over Spurs, one over Wolves and Wednesday and they were within two points of the leaders. Sheffield's good run had added one more team to what had been a three-horse race and there was all to play for.

---

**Nottingham Forest:** Thomson, Patrick, McDonald, Whitefoot, McKinlay, Burkett, Dwight, Gray, Iley, Younger, Imlach.
**Burnley:** Blacklaw, Angus, Marshall, Adamson, Cummings, Miller, Meredith, McIlroy, Pointer, Robson, Pilkington.

**Scorer:** Pointer.

# TENSE TIMES

**15 April 1960**
Referee: Mr L. McCoy

**Burnley 1 Leicester City 0**
Attendance: 23,777

Seven games to go and all to play for. The nerves were beginning to show in the young team, but they seemed to have put the drubbing by Wolves behind them as they began an Easter programme which saw them play four games in a week.

Chairman Bob Lord attacked Bobby Seith in the media, saying that the board 'will not stand for insubordination from any member of the club staff'. Bobby Seith, for his part, retained his dignity and said that he did not think any purpose would be served by a slanging match.

Leicester arrived at Turf Moor with ex-Claret Albert Cheeseborough. 'Cheesey' had, two years before, scored a hat-trick for Burnley in a 7-3 slaughtering of City. He'd almost scored four, cracking a shot from the centre circle which smacked against the post with the goalkeeper beaten – but that was two years ago.

There were to be no such feats in this match. Burnley had to win and Leicester had gone ten away games with only one defeat. This second defeat though was no fluke as the Clarets controlled the game for long periods and deserved more than the single goal.

For the second successive match the referee bemused fans of both teams with his decisions. Whereas Major Dennis in the Nottingham Forest game seemed incapable of getting a grip on the game, Mr McCoy seemed determined to get a grip, albeit by a circuitous route. After three minutes Burnley appeared to have scored when Gordon Banks – soon to star in the England World Cup winning squad – stumbled into the goal with the ball when trying to save a Robson header. The Burnley men celebrated but the referee waved play on.

Many fouls were awarded against Leicester and eventually Chalmers, who had persistently kicked McIlroy and Pilkington, had his name taken. For Leicester's part they relied on Cheeseborough to set up attacks, but he was well controlled throughout by Brian Miller. Leicester had only two chances of note, both of which fell to McDonald. Blacklaw was called upon to save several long distance shots and he performed his task competently and at times added a spectacular dive to his repertoire.

Tommy Cummings was a revelation. Cummings was the veteran of the side and he knew now that the Bobby Seith affair and the subsequent departure of Seith to Dundee meant that he was back in the team for the run-in. He was taking his chance with both hands – or should it be feet? – and he dominated the middle of the pitch again, reading every move and creating Burnley attacks out of defence with telling passes and shrewd runs.

# Burnley v. Leicester City

Billy White.

---

**Burnley:** Blacklaw, Angus, Elder, Adamson, Cummings, Miller, Connelly, McIlroy, Pointer, Robson, Pilkington.
**Leicester City:** Banks, Chalmers, Cunningham, McLintock, Knapp, Appleton, McDonald, Cheeseborough, Leek, Walsh.

**Scorer:** Connelly.

The goal which won the match was Connelly's 20th of the season and it was a cracker. Pilkington gained possession on the left wing and slipped the ball past Chalmers to Robson who, spotting that Chalmers had been left flatfooted, returned a pass to Pilky. Back to Robson then a stab to Connelly in the centre forward position. Connelly's shot whipped past Banks into the net and there was no return for the City.

Sadly, in the last seconds of the game, John Connelly was injured and lay prone for some time before the referee spotted him. It proved to be the end of Connelly's season and the start of a remarkable run for Trevor Meredith – who himself had been on the sidelines with a broken leg sustained in the opening match of the season! Burnley moved into third position with their victory.

Trevor Meredith.

# COME ON YOU CLARETS

**16 April 1960**                      **Burnley 3 Luton Town 0**
Referee: Mr A. Murdoch                 Attendance: 20,893

---

The visit of bottom club Luton Town was seen by the pundits as being an easy two points for Burnley and so it proved. The fact that Burnley only scored three should have been a source of great joy for Luton as the score could have reached double figures. The crowd against Luton was significant. Even though it was Easter and some fans were away on holiday an attendance figure of less than 21,000 was disappointing.

For the first five minutes of the game it looked as if nerves had caught up with the team and Cummings and Blacklaw forgot the basic rules of communication and almost gave a goal away. There followed a brief period of pressure and the nervous Burnley fans must have feared that it was going to be an off day – but the defence weathered the storm and from then on the Clarets yet again totally dominated their hapless opponents.

Tiny Trevor Meredith (even smaller than Brian Pilkington), played in place of England wing man John Connelly and he had a brilliant game. One of the national papers referred to him as 'the new Stanley Matthews'. Meredith was never a challenger to the great Stan, but his contribution to the Championship effort was, as it turned out, priceless. Meredith and Pilkington were the smallest wingers in the whole of the Football League.

The scoring was opened after fifteen minutes by Ray Pointer, who latched on to a loose ball from a Blacklaw clearance and netted from fully twenty yards when the defence felt he had no chance. Shortly after the goal, Pointer went down in a heap and was stretchered off. He returned for the second half but added little to the game and limped off for an X-ray. Fortunately nothing was broken and sighs of relief were heard around the pubs of Burnley the following day.

Luton, even with Burnley reduced to ten men, were outclassed and Burnley went on the rampage with McIlroy, Robson (twice), Pilkington and Miller having chances. Robson doubled the lead when Meredith embarked on a twisting run before laying on the pass for the inside left to convert.

Luton's goal led a charmed life. The Hatters could only stand and watch as the ball struck the post, the crossbar and the legs of desperate defenders – even full-backs Angus and Elder were making forays into enemy territory in an era when attacking backs were unheard of. It was Harry Potts' total football dream come to fruition. Months of painstaking training and attention to develop the skills of his young team were paying off.

Harry Potts, Burnley's manager.

---

**Burnley:** Blacklaw, Angus, Elder, Adamson, Cummings, Miller, Meredith, McIlroy, Pointer, Robson, Pilkington.
**Luton Town:** Baynham, Dunne, Hawks, Morton, Pacey, Brown, Bingham, Turner, McBride, Cummins, Noake.

**Scorers:** McIlroy, Pointer and Robson.

# BURNLEY v. LUTON TOWN

Jimmy Adamson.

Jimmy McIlroy was having a wonderful afternoon and he repeatedly mesmerised the defence, sometimes holding the ball, sometimes beating defenders with contemptuous ease and sometimes sending pinpoint passes half the length of the pitch to leave the white-shirted Luton players flatfooted. Pilkington on the left wing was running at – and beating – defenders at will and eventually Luton ran out of ideas and relied on two tactics, namely to kick the ball into touch and, if that failed, to kick the man into touch. In time, Mr Murdoch spoke severely to the Luton captain and the fouls became less.

Ironically, the third goal came from a penalty when Meredith was obstructed by Dunne and Hawks. Meredith dived theatrically and the referee pointed to the spot, from which Jimmy McIlroy stroked the ball home past Ron Baynham.

It was a scintillating display against the team which had appeared in the FA Cup final at Wembley less than twelve months previously and it firmly posted the ambitions of Burnley to the football world.

In the other top matches, Wolves lost to Newcastle United and Spurs were surprisingly beaten at home by Manchester City. Sheffield Wednesday dropped out of the race for the First Division championship with a 3-1 defeat at West Brom, so Burnley were in the strongest position of the top teams – even though the top place still eluded them. They were equal on points with Wolves and Spurs but lay in third position because of an inferior goal average. The missing piece of the puzzle was the fact that Burnley had a game in hand over Wolves and two in hand over Spurs. The talk of a Championship was in the air!

# CHEESEY BLUES

**18 April 1960**
Referee: Mr A.W. Sparling

**Leicester City 2 Burnley 1**
Attendance: 24,429

Disaster! All to play for and nerves froze – leaving Burnley three points behind Wolves and with three games out of their remaining four away from home. As is so often the case, irony played a part and Albert Cheeseborough, signed by Leicester from Burnley less than a year before, scored the hotly-disputed winner.

The Leicester team boasted no fewer than five changes from the meeting with Burnley three days before.

Pointer, appearing in spite of his injury, missed a golden chance in the opening seconds when he failed to find the target and his shot passed the post with Banks well beaten. That was about it in the first half for Burnley, in spite of a near own goal from Cunningham. The Clarets looked out of sorts and nervous and by the time the referee finally blew to signal the end of the first period the Filbert Street team had a two-goal advantage.

After half an hour Keyworth passed to Riley and his flick on found Wills, who shot home from twenty yards. The killer blow came when a through pass, again from man of the match Keyworth, found

Brian Pilkington.

# LEICESTER CITY v. BURNLEY

Adam Blacklaw.

**Leicester City:** Banks, Cunningham, Norman, White, Knapp, Appleton, Riley, Cheeseborough, Keyworth, Walsh, Wills.
**Burnley:** Blacklaw, Angus, Elder, Adamson, Cummings, Miller, Meredith, McIlroy, Pointer, Robson, Pilkington.

**Scorer:** Meredith.

Cheeseborough and the Burnley defence hesitated, waiting for an offside whistle. It was a fatal error and Cheeseborough scored what turned out to be the deciding goal.

The second period was an improvement and when Leicester's White miskicked a ball in his own area, Trevor Meredith was on hand and banged the ball home for his first Burnley goal. Burnley slung everything at the Midlanders and Gordon Banks gave an indication of the greatness that was yet to come. His best save came when one of his own defenders, centre half Knapp, miskicked and almost put the ball in the net from a few feet. At the other end, Cheeseborough again tormented his ex-colleagues when he burst out of defence and lashed a shot at goal which was saved by Blacklaw who tipped it over the bar.

Burnley looked tired after their full Easter programme and Leicester ran out worthy winners.

The Championship dream seemed to have gone. The top of the table read:

Wolves, played 40, points 52
Spurs,  played 40, points 49
Burnley, played 38, points 49

So Burnley had games in hand, but Wolves had scored 100 goals and, should the season end with the two teams equal on points, they would win the League on goal average. No-one really expected Wolves to drop a point and if this did turn out to be the case then Burnley needed to win all their remaining four games.

# BLOOMIN' BLOOMFIELD

**23 April 1960**
Referee: Mr K.R. Tuck

**Blackpool 1 Burnley 1**
Attendance: 23,753

Burnley knew that two points were vital from their visit to Bloomfield Road. They travelled without Adam Blacklaw, who had to miss the match due to injury, and Jim Furnell made his first appearance in goal. Furnell had replaced the unlucky Colin McDonald as reserve team goalkeeper and great things had been forecast for the local Clitheroe kid.

The seaside air did nothing for the nerves of the Burnley fans as mid-table Blackpool snatched a draw in the dying minutes to plunge the Claret followers into despair. Burnley were overanxious and their game was stilted and lacking in creativity.

For the second time in the season, Blackpool provided a stumbling block to the Burnley aspirations and, in truth, the Seasiders should have been well in command early on when Perry missed enough chances to score a hat-trick.

The pitch, a lumpy, dry mess, played its part as Burnley attacked the Blackpool goal and the ball shot off the turf – or rather the earth, as no grass was visible in

Dad takes charge at home. Brian Pilkington with his wife and baby at bath-time.

Meredith and Harris.

# BLACKPOOL v. BURNLEY

large patches – causing Blackpool to concede no fewer than twelve corners in the first half. In spite of their possession the Claret forward line never looked at ease, with the exception of Meredith and Pilkington on the wings. It was these two who combined for the Burnley goal. Pilkington took the corner and it was blocked by a defender and Meredith ran on to the rebound and smashed the ball past Waiters, leaving the Blackpool 'keeper without a chance.

It should have been the signal for Burnley to relax and dominate the game. Not so. Although the Clarets were clearly the better team, Blackpool kept fighting in a disorganised sort of way. It was when Hill came into the game wearing the famous Stanley Matthews' number 7 shirt that Burnley began to look rattled. Elder was having one of his rare off-days and Hill beat him comprehensively with only five minutes remaining and Charnley met the centre at the far post with a powerful header which beat defenders and goalkeeper alike.

It was a terribly disappointing result for the Burnley faithful but the big clash of the division, between leaders Wolves and second-placed Spurs had ended with a surprise result. Wolves had been deemed unbeatable at home and Spurs had been written off as the team which had lost its nerve in the last stage of the season. The result? Wolves 1, Spurs 3.

The top of the table read:

Wolves, played 41, points 52
Spurs, played 41, points 51
Burnley, played 39, points 50

The surprise at Molineux had let Burnley back in. The game was on again!

---

**Blackpool:** Waiters, Armfield, Martin, J. Kelly, Gratrix, Durie, Hill, Kaye, Charnley, Mudie, Perry.
**Burnley:** Furnell, Angus, Elder, Adamson, Cummings, Miller, Meredith, McIlroy, Pointer, Robson, Pilkington.

**Scorer:** Meredith.

# GOING TO THE TAPE

**27 April 1960**
Referee: Mr R.E. Smith

**Birmingham City 0 Burnley 1**
Attendance: 37,014

The injury problems were piling up at the death. Connelly was definitely out and on the day before the match there were doubts over Miller, McIlroy and Cummings. In the end they all played in the vital game at St Andrews.

The long-suffering fans had to wait until the 81st minute for Pilkington to score the goal which brought Burnley equal on points with Wolves. The team suffered again from nerves – the defence looked jittery and the attack disjointed. Fortunately for them, Birmingham were fighting to avoid relegation; they too were not at their best and both teams seemed unable to overcome the pitch conditions.

McIlroy came close to scoring with a blasted free-kick which was deflected by Schofield. Burnley had the lion's share of the game and the Claret-festooned fans rose to their feet when Pointer 'scored' only to lapse into disgruntled silence when they realised that the referee had disallowed the goal for offside. More disappointment came when Meredith was upended in the penalty area and Mr Smith gave an indirect free-kick.

The second half opened with a mini-comedy as Pilkington charged at goal-keeper Schofield and ripped the goalkeeper's shorts so badly that they had to be replaced by the trainer. Pilkington was roundly booed thereafter.

Some of the tackles were diabolical, with studs being flashed dangerously but no one was seriously hurt as Burnley began to pile on the pressure. Then it was Birmingham's turn and they swept forward in blue waves and laid siege to the Burnley goal. The game swung from end to end and the pace was frenetic, causing shots to be missed and mistakes to be made. The tension on and off the pitch was palpable.

Then, with nine minutes remaining, Meredith shook off a high tackle from Farmer and with great aplomb slipped the ball cheekily through the legs of Neal and centred. What happened next seemed to be in slow motion. Everyone expected Pointer to trap the ball and shoot but instead he flicked it on to Pilkington and Pilkington rapped it home. Brian Pilkington claimed that when the shot hit the net he screamed 'What a relief!'

The last nine minutes were constant Birmingham pressure and Brian Miller made a vital goal-line clearance and Adamson, who had been calm, composed and authoritative throughout, continued to break down the Birmingham threat. Adamson on this night showed why he should have played for England. He was the master of every situation and showed why his captaincy was such a vital part of Burnley's challenge.

# BIRMINGHAM CITY v. BURNLEY

Alex Elder.

**Birmingham:** Schofield, Sissons, Farmer, Watts, Smith, Neal, Astall, Gordon, Weston, Murphy, Hooper.
**Burnley:** Blacklaw, Angus, Elder, Adamson, Cummings, Miller, Meredith, McIlroy, Pointer, Robson, Pilkington.

**Scorer:** Pilkington.

Adam Blacklaw.

# STUNNED

**30 April 1960**
Referee: Mr A. Holland

**Burnley 0 Fulham 0**
Attendance: 29,856

The last home game of the season and two points vital. In the event one point was dropped. It was a dreadful display, full of nerves and indecision, and it left us stunned. So poor was the performance in fact, that many of us believed that the Championship was already lost. Staggeringly, less than 30,000 turned up – over 22,000 less than the fifth round cup tie against lowly Bradford City!

Tony Macedo, Fulham's goalkeeper, had an inspired day. He was well known as an acrobatic 'keeper and he appeared calm and collected throughout the match, as did his Fulham colleagues. Burnley, on the other hand, ran around like headless chickens, desperate to create an opening – but on the day lacking the skills to do so.

The game contained few moments of great note and Fulham seemed content to simply play out the season and watch the Clarets run in ever decreasing circles. The lack of a general was apparent. Adamson tried to slow things down and again he was the man of the match – along with the revitalised Tommy Cummings. They both nullified the effect of Johnny Haynes and, as a contest, the game was a dead duck.

Elsewhere, Wolves had beaten Chelsea at Stamford Bridge and Tottenham Hotspur had done what Burnley had failed to do and crushed Blackpool at home. It was a dispirited Burnley camp at twenty to five in the afternoon of 13 April and a strangely silent crowd filtered out of Turf Moor.

Wolves and Spurs had both finished their League programme and Burnley had one to play, at Maine Road against Manchester City.

The table read:

Wolves 54 points
Spurs  53 points
Burnley 53 points

Burnley *had* to win the last game of the season. After this display few people gave them much chance. What they had forgotten was that Jimmy McIlroy was absent through injury. Could his return be a signal for the much needed return to form?

Whatever the situation, the retreating crowd from Turf Moor had, due to their disappointment, forgotten that they could be just one game away from a League Championship.

John Angus.

---

**Burnley:** Blacklaw, Angus, Elder, Adamson, Cummings, Miller, Meredith, Lawson, Pointer, Robson, Pilkington.
**Fulham:** Macedo, Cohen, Langley, Mullery, Bentley, Lowe, Key, O'Connell, Doherty, Haynes, Chamberlain.

# MAINE ROAD MAYHEM

2 May 1960                                    Manchester City 1 Burnley 2
Referee: Mr T.H. Gerrard                      Attendance: 65,981

Burnley arrived at Maine Road for their ninth game in a month. It had been a punishing schedule. Now, when only a win would bring the Championship to Lancashire, the pressure was intense. Would the young team have the nerve to win?

Over 65,000 fans crammed into Maine Road, in contrast to the 30,000 who had watched Burnley's last home game. Alec Farmer, a young off-duty Burnley policeman, made his way to Manchester with a group of colleagues and arrived to find that the ground was full and the gates were locked. A young man climbed over and opened the gates from the inside and the crowd surged in. Alec was swept from the steps outside to halfway down the terraces before he could stop. He recalls that if just one person had tripped there would have been a major disaster. Happily no one was seriously hurt.

Still living in Burnley and a season ticket holder in the Bob Lord Stand, Alec was in hospital awaiting a serious operation when I talked to him about the famous night. He sat quietly as he cast his mind back and a smile played on his lips. 'The excitement was so great. Nerves were stretched so much that I don't remember much about the game itself' he said in a soft Scottish accent ' ...but I can recall the atmosphere as if it were yesterday. If we failed to win then Wolverhampton Wanderers would win the League title for the third successive year. I think we all feared the worst after the Blackpool and Fulham games.'

Wolves were the glamour team of the 1950s and if they did win their third successive Championship they would equal the feat last achieved by Arsenal in 1935. Wolves manager Stan Cullis was in the crowd and many thousands – some of them Wolves fans – were locked out of the dangerously overcrowded Maine Road.

Doubts that Burnley had the stomach or nerve for the fight were soon dispelled. Gone was the lethargy of the Fulham display and the Clarets battled for every ball. For the umpteenth time, Burnley found themselves playing on a bumpy pitch with many brown, bald areas. It was totally unsuited to Burnley's cultured style and dictated that this was an occasion for a fight rather than for pure football. Burnley were not found wanting. Nerves were showing at the start with the Clarets avoiding any mistakes. City too appeared to be overawed by the occasion.

Manchester were full of energy if not direction and they played with such ferocity that an uninformed observer might have thought that it was the light blues who were fighting to take the Championship. Any Burnley fan who thought that City would give way to their Lancashire neighbours at the expense of Wolves were sadly mistaken.

The match was only four minutes old when the City fans were stunned into silence and the Claret contingent erupted. Burnley gained a throw in, Elder received the ball and passed to Robson who distributed it speedily to Pilkington. Pilky cut in from the wing and hit a hard low centre across the goal mouth. Trautmann, the heroic German goalkeeper, had misjudged his position and the ball entered the net via the far post.

City launched themselves at Burnley, leaving great gaps at the back which weren't capitalised upon. Trautmann made amends with two fine saves when Burnley counterattacked and then disaster struck. The young Dennis Law seemed to be in an offside position but the referee waved play on. Law tried to flick the ball towards goal but made a hash of it and only half connected. It dropped conveniently for Hayes who slammed it home.

1-1 and not a fingernail left. The tension amongst the fans was masked by a wall of sound urging the ball into the City net.

McIlroy shouldn't have been playing at all and he was heavily strapped up. He tried to slow the frenetic pace but City would have none of it and the bone-shaking tackles continued. Even so, Burnley made chances and the German goalkeeper was again at his brilliant best when he reached a Robson effort with his fingertips and turned it over.

Ewing flattened Pointer with a dreadful challenge. Cummings took the resulting free-kick to the left of goal and after a brief skirmish Branagan tried to clear but succeeded only in slicing the ball to Meredith. The crowd seemed to hold its collective breath as Trevor Meredith scored what was arguably Burnley's most famous goal by slamming the ball past Trautmann and just inside the post.

Burnley gained a greater control in the second half, even though Dennis Law was trying desperately to weave his magic. Cummings and Adamson led from the back, captain and ex-captain in one accord for the claret cause as Burnley held on to the lead and almost increased it – a brilliant bicycle kick was saved by Trautmann when the whole ground thought it was a goal.

---

**Manchester City:** Trautmann, Branagan, Sear, Barnes, Ewing, Oakes, Barlow, Hannah, Hayes, Law, Colbridge.
**Burnley:** Blacklaw, Angus, Elder, Adamson, Cummings, Miller, Meredith, McIlroy, Pointer, Robson, Pilkington.

**Scorers:** Pilkington and Meredith.

# Manchester City v. Burnley

The match swung from end to end and the Burnley fans looked anxiously at their watches. Law broke through and seemed certain to score before he was dispossessed by Adamson. Jimmy McIlroy at the other end set Pilkington free with a couple of minutes left but the diminutive winger was limping from an injury and failed to control the ball.

The Burnley supporters created a chorus of whistles to remind Mr Gerrard that the match only lasted ninety minutes but still play continued. A tired lob by Trautmann started another City attack but the claret-shirted defenders snuffed out the threat. Some spectators turned away, unable to bear the tension any longer. Others stood, fists clenched and biting bottom lips.

The whistle!

It was over! Burnley, the small-town Lancashire club were Champions of the Football League! The Burnley support erupted in a cacophony of joyful sound. The unbearable tension was over. The heart-stopping ride had reached its end. Alec recalled the journey back to Burnley as hundreds of cars waited for the team coach and followed it through the night back home. He summed it up in a few words: 'We followed the coach all the way back. It was like a flotilla of tugs following a liner. It was wonderful, just wonderful.'

From left to right: Adamson, Pointer, Blacklaw and Cummings.

The BiblioGov Project is an effort to expand awareness of the public documents and records of the U.S. Government via print publications. In broadening the public understanding of government and its work, an enlightened democracy can grow and prosper. Ranging from historic Congressional Bills to the most recent Budget of the United States Government, the BiblioGov Project spans a wealth of government information. These works are now made available through an environmentally friendly, print-on-demand basis, using only what is necessary to meet the required demands of an interested public. We invite you to learn of the records of the U.S. Government, heightening the knowledge and debate that can lead from such publications.

Included are the following Collections:

Budget of The United States Government
Presidential Documents
United States Code
Education Reports from ERIC
GAO Reports
History of Bills
House Rules and Manual
Public and Private Laws

Code of Federal Regulations
Congressional Documents
Economic Indicators
Federal Register
Government Manuals
House Journal
Privacy act Issuances
Statutes at Large

# Oil Spills in U.S. Coastal Waters: Background, Governance, and Issues for Congress

Jonathan L. Ramseur